The Multiple Case Study Design

Most organizations today operate in volatile economic and social environments and qualitative research plays an essential role in investigating leadership and management problems. This unique volume offers novice and experienced researchers a brief, student-centric research methods text specifically devoted to the multiple case study design.

The multiple case study design is a valuable qualitative research tool in studying the links between the personal, social, behavioral, psychological, organizational, cultural, and environmental factors that guide organizational and leadership development. Case study research is essential for the in-depth study of participants' perspectives on the phenomenon within its natural context. Rigorously designed management and leadership case studies in the extant literature have a central focus on individual managers' and leaders' stories and their perceptions of the broader forces operating within and outside their organizations.

This is a comprehensive methodology book exploring the multiple case study design with step-by-step and easily accessible guidelines on the topic, making it especially valuable to researchers, academics, and students in the areas of business, management, and leadership.

Daphne Halkias is Professor and Distinguished Research Fellow at École des Ponts Business School in Paris, France.

Michael Neubert is Associate Professor in Business and Management Studies and a Member of the Academic Council at UIBS in Zurich, Switzerland.

Paul W. Thurman is Professor of Management and Analytics at Columbia University's Mailman School of Public Health, New York, USA.

Nicholas Harkiolakis is on the Faculty of the School of Technology at Northcentral University, San Diego, California, USA.

Routledge Focus on Business and Management

The fields of business and management have grown exponentially as areas of research and education. This growth presents challenges for readers trying to keep up with the latest important insights. *Routledge Focus on Business and Management* presents small books on big topics and how they intersect with the world of business research.

Individually, each title in the series provides coverage of a key academic topic, whilst collectively, the series forms a comprehensive collection across the business disciplines.

South African Business in China
Navigating Institutions
Kelly Meng

Privatisation in India
Journey and Challenges
Sudhir Naib

Global Financialization and Corporate Innovation Strategy
The Case of Korean Firms
Hwan Joo Seo and Sung Jin Kang

The Multiple Case Study Design
Methodology and Application for Management Education
Daphne Halkias, Michael Neubert, Paul W. Thurman and Nicholas Harkiolakis

For more information about this series, please visit: www.routledge.com/Routledge-Focus-on-Business-and-Management/book-series/FBM

The Multiple Case Study Design

Methodology and Application for Management Education

Daphne Halkias, Michael Neubert, Paul W. Thurman and Nicholas Harkiolakis

Routledge
Taylor & Francis Group

NEW YORK AND LONDON

First published 2022
by Routledge
605 Third Avenue, New York, NY 10158

and by Routledge
4 Park Square, Milton Park, Abingdon, Oxon, OX14 4RN

Routledge is an imprint of the Taylor & Francis Group, an informa business

Library of Congress Cataloging-in-Publication Data
A catalog record for this title has been requested

ISBN: 978-1-032-15608-8 (hbk)
ISBN: 978-1-032-15610-1 (pbk)
ISBN: 978-1-003-24493-6 (ebk)

DOI: 10.4324/9781003244936

Typeset in Times New Roman
by Newgen Publishing UK

Contents

About the Authors

Daphne Halkias, PhD, is Professor and Distinguished Research Fellow at École des Ponts Business School in Paris, France; a Fellow at Institute of Coaching, McLean Hospital at Harvard Medical School; Faculty at International Business School Paris; Research Affiliate at the Institute for Social Sciences, Cornell University; Research Associate at the Center for Comparative Immigration Studies, University of California, San Diego. Dr. Halkias is CEO of Executive Coaching Consultants and Editor of *International Journal of Teaching and Case Studies*, *International Journal of Technology Enhanced Learning*, and *International Journal of Social Entrepreneurship and Innovation*. She is a member of the Academy of Management, Business Fights Poverty, the American Psychological Association, and Family Firm Institute, to name a few. She is the author of 12 academic books and over 100 peer-reviewed papers.

Michael Neubert, PhD, is Associate Professor in Business and Management Studies and a Member of the Academic Council at UIBS in Zurich, Switzerland. He teaches international business and finance modules on the undergraduate, graduate, and postgraduate level. His current research interests are: Multiple Case Study Research Designs, Live Teaching Case Studies, Internationalization Speed, Dynamic Pricing, and FinTech. He regularly publishes his research findings in peer-reviewed journals and has co-authored several books (e.g., *The Innovative Business School*, 2020 by Routledge). Dr. Neubert is also the founder and CEO of C2NM LLC, a Swiss consulting and software developing firm, which helps its clients to enter foreign markets more efficiently through the use of predictive data analytics and artificial intelligence.

Paul W. Thurman, DBA, a Columbia MBA valedictorian, service award winner, and multiple teaching award recipient, has extensive advisory and management experience helping a variety of Fortune 500 firms realize value from innovative business, operations, and technology strategies. Professor Thurman currently teaches strategic management and data analysis courses at Columbia's Mailman School of Public Health. In addition to his faculty appointments, Professor Thurman serves as a clinical professor and affiliated researcher at the National Cancer Institute's Center for Cancer Research at the National Institutes of Health. His peer-reviewed research has focused on scientific collaboration and its effect on research quality, and also on cancer drug patents, FDA approvals, and market pricing. He recently published his 11th book, a research compendium on evolving business school teaching and research models.

Nicholas Harkiolakis, PhD, is on the Faculty of School of Technology at Northcentral University, San Diego, California, USA. Dr. Harkiolakis is an internationally recognized researcher and author in research methods, leadership, and e-negotiations, with over 25 years of experience in the organizational development of E-Business, E-Commerce, IS/IT management, and strategy. He has been involved at the executive level in technology, education start-ups, and consulting in the IS/IT area. After a distinguished international academic and research career, Dr. Harkiolakis is Executive Vice President Director of Research and Innovative Technology Projects at Executive Coaching Consultants, developing cutting-edge research studies and programs with global corporate and academic partners.

Preface: The Multiple Case Study Design as a Valuable Research Tool

Qualitative research plays an essential role in investigating leadership and management problems, given that they remain complex social enigmas even after tons of ink has been spilled on behalf of these phenomena for longer than anyone cares to remember. Quantitative methods remain insufficient to investigate a phenomenon that bears dynamic and symbolic components at multiple levels. Qualitative methods support investigators to interpret contexts in which leadership is defined through daily lived experiences.

Denzin and Lincoln (2005) wrote that qualitative researchers follow an interpretive and naturalistic approach: 'This means that qualitative researchers study things in their natural settings, attempting to make sense of, or interpret, phenomena in terms of the meanings people bring to them' (p. 3). Researchers within the leadership and management discipline are increasingly adopting qualitative methods in their studies mainly because of the approach's flexibility and suitability in capturing the multiple dimensions of subtle differences in social phenomena (Halkias et al., 2017).

The multiple case study design is a valuable research tool in studying the links between the personal, social, behavioral, psychological, organizational, cultural, and environmental factors that guide organizational and leadership development (Abadir et al., 2020). Case study research is essential for the in-depth study of participants' perspectives on a phenomenon within its natural context. Rigorously designed management and leadership case studies in the extant literature have a central focus on individual managers' and leaders' stories and their perceptions of the broader forces operating within and outside their organizations.

Extant theories can be expanded and enhanced with a multiple case study design to gather data to answer a qualitative research question. Using a multiple case study design, the extension of theory can contribute value to a particular theoretical perspective and further define the original theory's boundaries. Multiple cases are like multiple experiments, to which the previously developed theory can be compared and extended to account for the empirical results of the case study (Yin, 2017). Examining the rich data collected in theoretically significant cases can bring additional constructs and relationships to reflect the actual multiple case study data set. Extension studies provide replication evidence and support extending prior research results by offering new and critical theoretical directions (Bonett, 2012).

Theory extension from a multiple case study is distinct from other theory-building approaches, such as mathematical modeling or computational simulation. Using a multiple case study design, the theory extension is guided by logic informed by empirical data's systematic analysis. Theory extension through multiple case study research is a broader approach than other inductive methods such as *interpretivist research*, where knowledge is assumed to be socially constructed by study participants' voices and lived experiences (Cooper & White, 2012).

Narrative and phenomenological studies often focus on exploring constructs such as identity, the meaning of experience, participant voice, and socially constructed knowledge about a specific phenomenon and less on creating theory extension. Ethnography researchers explore culture through immersive observation and daily practices often unbeknown to the observed participants, such as non-verbal cues, cultural rituals, and data derived from artifacts. Nevertheless, qualitative approaches such as multiple case, interpretivist, and ethnographic studies utilize common research strategies such as immersion in the phenomenon studied and purposeful sampling.

Both novice and experienced qualitative researchers can use multiple case studies to contribute original qualitative data to extant theory. Although a qualitative study's exploratory nature overrules a theoretical framework's benefits, theory-free research does not exist (Guba & Lincoln, 1994). A researcher who cannot formulate a theoretical framework to ground their multiple case study still needs to immerse themselves in the literature to further discover preconceptions about their study.

Findings in a multiple case study can confirm or extend the existing knowledge in the discipline as each case presented can be grounded in the reviewed literature (Stake, 2010). Multiple case study research is beneficial for responding to "How" and "Why" questions and what Eisenhardt (1989, 2020) terms as "big picture" research questions that essentially are broad inquiries to address a gap in the extant litera-ture. When a research question is tightly bound within the context of an existing theory, using a set of multiple, theoretically relevant case studies to understand complex processes in this theory is deemed the goal of rigorous, multiple case study research.

1 A Refresher on the Philosophical Foundations of Academic Research

The origin of the word research can be traced to the French *recherché* (to seek out) as a composite, suggesting a repeated activity (*re*) of searching (*cherché*). Going even further, we arrive at its Latin root in the form of *circare* (to wander around) and eventually to circle. This wandering around in some cyclical fashion is intuitive, as we will see later on, since it accurately reflects the process we follow in modern research. The only exception is that the circles are getting deeper and deeper into what the "real" world reveals to us. Noticing the quotes around the word "real" might have revealed the direction we will follow here in challenging what "real" means and accepting how it affects the process we follow when we investigate a research topic.

Concerns about the nature of reality are vital in deciding about the nature of truth and the ways to search for it. This brings us to the realm of philosophy or, more specifically, its branch of metaphysics, where we deal with questions of existence. Explaining the world and understanding its function (to the extent possible) allow us to accept what is real and make sense of it. Our perception of the metaphysical worldview is the cause of our behavior and for moving on in life. Questions about the origin of the universe belong to the branch of metaphysics called cosmology, while questions about the nature of reality and the state of being are the concern of the branch of metaphysics called ontology. The latter is essential to the way we approach and conduct research as it provides a foundation for describing what exists and the truth about the objects of research.

In addition to the issues about the reality that research needs to address based on our ontological stance, there are epistemological assumptions that guide our approach to learning. These address issues about what knowledge is—what we can know and how we learn. These questions, of course, are based on the assumption that knowledge about

DOI: 10.4324/9781003244936-1

the world can be acquired in an "objective"/real way, connecting in this way with ontology. As we will soon see, the interplay between epistemology and ontology is reflected in the different research traditions adopted and guide past and present research efforts as they determine the theory and methods utilized in conducting research.

The ontological and epistemological stances we adopt are considered paradigms and reflect the researcher's understanding of the nature of existence from first principles beyond "logical" debate. As paradigms, they are accepted as self-sufficient logical constructs (dogmas in a way) that are beyond the scrutiny of proof or doubt. Selecting one is more of an intuitive leap of faith than an "objective" process of logical and empirical conclusions. Both ontology and epistemology are tightly related to what can be called the "theory of truth." This is an expression of how arguments connect the various concepts we adopt in research and the conditions that make these arguments true or false depending on the ontological and epistemological posture we adopt. In that respect, arguments can represent concepts, intentions, conditions, correlations, and causations that we accept as true or false with a certain degree of confidence.

Typical theories of truth include the instrumentalist, coherence, and correspondence theories. The last reflects the classical representations that Plato and Aristotle adopted where something is true when it "reflects" reality. This posture can be heavily challenged in the world of social sciences since individuals' perceptions vary and can suggest different views of reality, making it impossible to have a universal agreement on social "facts." Such perceptions can influence how beliefs fit together (cohere) in producing an explanation of the phenomenon we are investigating. This is also the basic posture of coherence theory, which postulates that truth is interpretation-oriented and constructed in social settings.

The instrumentalist view of truth emphasizes interrelations between truth and action and connects the positive outcomes of an action to the truth behind the intention that led to that action. This is more of a results-oriented perception of truth and the basis of the pragmatist epistemology, as we will see later on. In terms of supporting theories, research can be descriptive, like when we make factual claims of what leaders and organizations do, instrumental, like when we study the impact and influence of behavior, and normative, when we try to provide evidence that supports a particular direction. For each one of these "categories" of research, ontology and epistemology are there to provide philosophical grounds and guidance.

Before delving into the philosophical foundations of academic research, novice researchers must often confuse the terms *method* and *methodology*. The methodology commonly refers to the frame of reference on which the inquiry method is based and it is typically subjected to a specific set of guiding principles and justifies using a particular research method. Guba and Lincoln (1989) define methodology as the 'overall strategy for resolving the complete set of choices and options available to the inquirer' (p. 183). A research *method* describes the most suitable way to collect and analyze data within the study context. A case study as a method examines particular "cases," including individuals and events. Using multiple data sources and collection methods, a case study explores and critiques a phenomenon in context (i.e., bound). It is possible that, as a conceptual definition, qualitative case studies could potentially be both a method and a methodology, depending on the underpinning philosophy.

Ontology

Of particular research interest is ontology, the branch of metaphysics that deals with the nature of being and existence or, in simplified terms, what reality is. Although it is not clear what reality is and how it relates to other things, one can always resolve to degrees of belief that ensure commitment to answers and, by extension, acceptance of a particular theory of the world. In this way, an ontological stance will provide an acceptable dogma of how the world is built and, more specifically, concerning social sciences, which we are interested in here, the nature of the social phenomenon under investigation.

Realism. Realism's premise is that the world exists regardless of who observes it. In our case, this means that the universe existed before us and will continue to exist after we are gone (not just as individuals but also as a species). The philosophical positions of realism have been quite controversial as they can be accepted or rejected in parts according to one's focus. Many variations of realism have been developed from various philosophical schools to address deviations from the generic realist path. Among them, critical realism, idealism, and internal realism hold prominent positions. The first two have been going at each other for some time now as rivals of realism. Critical realists insist on separating social and physical objects because social structures cannot exist in isolation and are derivatives of the activities they govern and their agents' perceptions. In turn, these structures tend to influence the perceptions of their agents, creating in this sense a closed system between agents and their social construct. Idealists critique the positions of critical realists by suggesting their interpretations and subject of inquiry fall into metaphysics as they construct imaginary entities that further impose an ideology that, like most ideologies, can be oppressive and exploitable.

Relativism. Relativism takes an opposite stance to realism by assuming that what we perceive as reality is nothing more than the product of conventions and frameworks of assessment that we have popularized and agreed as representing the truth. In that sense, truth is a human fabrication, and no one assessment of human conduct is more valid than another. Understanding is context- and location-specific, and rationality, among others, is the subject of research rather than an undisputed conceptual resource for researchers. Relativists view reality as time-dependent. Something that was considered accurate at some time could easily be proven false at a later time when experience and resources reveal another aspect of the phenomenon or situation under investigation. Research provides revelations of reality and discourses help develop practices and representations that help us experience and make sense of the world.

Epistemology. The etymology of the word epistemology suggests the discourse about the formal observation and acquisition of knowledge. As sources of knowledge, we consider "reliable" ones like testimonies, memory, reason, perception, and introspection and exclude volatile forms like desires, emotions, prejudice, and biases. Perception through our five senses is the primary entry point of information into the mind where it can be retained in memory for further processing through reason. Testimony is an indirect form of knowledge after which we rely on someone else to provide credible information about someone or something else. Finally, introspection, as a unique capacity of humans to inspect their thinking, can supplement reason in making decisions about the nature of evidence and truth.

For the academic research that we are interested in here, epistemology is vital in defining our approach to data collection and analysis and interpreting findings in search of the underlining truth of the phenomenon we are studying. A more practical perspective that is also of interest to research concerns creating and disseminating knowledge in a domain of study. Again, as we did with the case of ontology, we will discuss here the primary schools of thought that guide social sciences research, like positivism and constructivism. In positivism, as we will see next, the social world exists in reality, and we try to accurately represent it as knowledge, while in constructivism, learning takes place in a social context as we confirm our knowledge with others.

Positivism. Positivism is based on the idea that the social world exists externally and can be studied and represented accurately by human knowledge only when validated empirically. This aligns well with the realist perspective and the corresponding theory of truth, but it should not be seen as one-to-one correspondence. Social entities and their interactions are seen as observables that can be expressed through appropriate parameters and variables. These can be studied and empirically tested to reveal the true nature of social phenomena. For example, organizational structure and culture exist and can be studied to provide proof of their influence on organizational performance.

Constructivism. Constructivism is applied in response to the "absolute" nature of learning through observation of and experimentation with measurable entities to address the subjective nature of social experience and interaction. In the constructivist paradigm, it is argued that our perception of the world is a social construct formed by commonly agreed beliefs among people and that these constructs should be investigated by research. We assume here that the internal beliefs of individuals shape their perceptions of their external reality to the extent that they behave as if their constructed reality is the actual reality, making the argument about an objective reality unimportant.

The way people communicate and express their beliefs and positions and understand what drives them to interact the way they do takes here the place of a cause-and-effect relationship that, in other approaches, forms the basis for understanding and explaining phenomena. Social interactions are not a direct response to external stimuli but develop an agreed-upon meaning before materializing a reaction. The grounds upon which constructivism is developed align it almost perfectly with relativism. A significant challenge with constructivism regarding research is that an external perspective is required when dealing with external events, like how the market behaves or how an organization interacts with its stakeholders. The issue is no longer how we perceive reality but rather what the reality of external stakeholders is. Another challenge we face is the inability to compare views of individuals as they are subjectively formed and do not represent accurate/realistic reflections of their outside world.

To address many of the challenges constructivists face concerning quality (like validity in positivism), compliance with a set of criteria is sought in constructivism-based research. Prominent among them is authenticity, whereby the researchers need to understand the issue under investigation. Additionally, they need to demonstrate their impartiality in interpreting findings as expert methodologists. In that direction, identifying correct operational measures for the concepts being studied will support construct validity. Internal and external validity are also of concern as they aim to establish causal relationships and ensure the transferability of findings.

2 Research Methodologies
The Basics

Armed with our beliefs about the nature of reality and learning, we adopt the process we will follow in collecting information and data about the phenomenon we will study. As a field of study, methodology concerns the systematic study and analysis of the methods used for observations and concluding. In short, the methodology is the philosophy of methods and encompasses the rules for reaching valid conclusions (epistemology) and the domains/"objects" (ontology) of investigation that form an observable phenomenon. Its philosophical roots suggest that it is expressed as an attitude toward inquiry and learning grounded in our perception of reality and forms our behavior's guiding principles.

For example, a positivist perspective would assume that burnout exists in reality and formulate tests using large samples to measure it and confirm its existence while providing details of the various variables and parameters influencing its expression. In this way, a cause-and-effect relationship will be established between the individual influencers/variables. One could find control variables like the environment (suppressive and authoritarian) and independent variables (we will talk about them soon) like genetic predisposition. The focus during data collection and analysis is more on observations of the phenomenon "What," "When," "Where," and "Who" and the "How" and "Why" as generalizations during the interpretation and conclusions phase.

On the other side of positivism, we can consider a constructivist perspective that would focus on aspects of the environment individuals consider as contributing to burnout and how they manage themselves in such situations. Researchers would arrange for interviews with those who have experienced burnout. By recording the individuals' stories and appropriate probing about the phenomenon, the researcher develops themes that persist across individuals and explain the phenomenon's surfaces. The focus here is more on the "How" and "Why" and leaves

DOI: 10.4324/9781003244936-2

the identification of commonalities "What," "When," "Where," and "Who" for the interpretation and conclusions. In a way, it is like going from *effect* to *cause*, while in positivism, the perspective will move from *cause* to *effect*. A point of interest here is that the researcher does not define the phenomenon and its characteristics but leaves it up to the research subjects.

It is worth pointing out what a phenomenon is, as we frequently refer to it as the core element or the essence of research. By its etymology, a phenomenon is something that appears, meaning it is observed. In our case, we will also add the element of repeated appearance; otherwise, it might not deserve the effort one can devote to its study. Value from research comes from the understanding we gain about something that we can later use to make predictions and optimally deal with similar situations. Understanding comes from representing the complexity of what we observe with abstract representations (variables, constructs, parameters), their classification according to their similarities and proximity to other abstractions, and how they interconnect and react to each other.

If we can identify the various elements of the phenomenon with precision and detail enough to measure them as specific quantities, we can say that our data are quantitative, and thus the methodology we will follow is a **quantitative** one. Such quantities include age, gender, education level, etc. On the other hand, our observations concern constructs that cannot accurately be represented as quantities. We can say that our research requires a **qualitative** methodology. Such constructs include feelings, beliefs, perceptions, etc. If both quantitative and qualitative elements are required to describe and explain a phenomenon accurately, then a combination of methods (**mixed** methods) would be the recommended path.

Quantitative Methodologies

The quantitative method and analysis are based on meaning derived from numerical form data like scale scores, ratings, durations, counts, etc. This is in contrast to qualitative methods, where meaning is derived from narratives. The quantitative research numbers can come directly from observation or indirectly by converting collected information into a numerical form (like a Likert scale, which we will see later). While this definition of quantitative research covers the basics of what it is, a more in-depth representation defines quantitative methodologies as an attempt to measure (positivist stance mainly) an objective reality (realist stance mainly). We assume that the phenomenon under study is natural (not a social construct) and can be represented (knowable) by estimating parameters and measuring meaningful variables representing the state of entities involved in the phenomenon under study (Harkiolakis, 2017).

Associations among such variables can further establish relationships and ultimately suggest cause and effect to predict the value of one variable (effect) based on another's observations (cause). This process is particularly suited when we form hypotheses to explain something. Hypotheses are statements of truth about facts that an investigation can further test. This usually follows when theories or models are formed to provide "solid" (statistically, that is) evidence of their statement and assertions. Model testing is otherwise the domain of the quantitative research methodology.

To produce results with high reliability, quantitative research requires a large sample of participants, and the analysis is done through statistical tools. Large samples ensure better representativeness and generalizability of findings and the proper application of the statistical tests. The investigator and the investigated are independent entities, and, therefore, the investigator can study a phenomenon without influencing it or being influenced by it. This ensures an objective treatment of the collected data, increasing the reliability of the study. Facts are separated from values, and the "truth" of what is observed is the external reality of the observation. This is also supported by the rigid procedures that need to be followed during data collection that ensure reliable measurement eliminates the researcher's potential biases and personal values.

Collecting data for quantitative studies is based on instruments and procedures. The former concerns the development of written forms for collecting information through observation and surveys, while the latter concerns the proper steps to collect information. Since data come in numerical form, mathematical methods (like statistics) are recruited for their processing. We should clarify that while some variables are numerical (like weight, age, revenue, income, etc.), others (like quality, performance, beliefs, attitudes, etc.) might need to have some scale developed for their measurement. For the latter category, a questionnaire might be developed where a measure of agreement with a statement (like "strongly disagree," "disagree," "neither agree nor disagree," "agree," "strongly agree") can be selected by participants. This type of scale will be "assumed" (more on this when we discuss surveys) equivalent to a numerical scale (like "strongly disagree" = 1, "disagree" = 2, etc.).

Using structured instruments in quantitative research requires standardization of procedures to ensure replicability to confirm findings. Credibility is ensured, and universality of the proof (model of the phenomenon under investigation) is enforced as long as contrary evidence is not revealed. While the great advantage of quantitative methods is establishing proof about dependencies and the existence of relations among quantities that are easy to replicate and generalize, the methodology is not free of criticism. A disadvantage of quantitative methods is that it is frequently unclear what the answers to questions (in polls, for example) mean regarding the subjects' behavior. In other words, the contextual details of a situation are not easily captured, primarily when attitudes, beliefs, and behavior, in general, are studied. This is something that quantitative researchers usually defend by emphasizing that the focus of quantitative methods is not on what behavior means but on what causes it and its explanation.

Qualitative Methodologies

While forming generalized results, quantitative methods do not serve as direct observations of a phenomenon. The researchers are usually in control of the environment, so the results are seen to an extent as "laboratory results" instead of "life observations." Using instruments like questionnaires is considered intervention and considered expressions of the designers/researchers rather than independent and objective measurement instruments. In general, a qualitative methodology is defined as everything that is not quantitative. While this definition by exclusion might reflect a great extent of the truth, it is best to define what is qualitative research instead of what is not. In search of a definition of qualitative research, the word quality's roots can serve as a point of departure.

Quality comes with many meanings, ranging from the essence of something to something concerning another/similar something taken as a standard. By "something," in the context of research, we refer to theoretical constructs that represent assemblies of conceptual elements that appear as independent entities influencing or representing phenomena or aspects of them. In that respect, the first definition of quality can form the basis upon which qualitative methodology is expressed. While the latter definition might seem irrelevant to a research methodology, this is far from the truth.

Qualitative research is grounded on comparing theoretical constructs as it is in comparing that new constructs are developed. Such constructs are necessary for social sciences when human behavior needs to be studied. Needs move humans, and in response to environmental triggers (both physical and social), they build an understanding of the world around them that helps them make sense of it and respond. One definition that captures all this is to see qualitative research as a methodology that aims to understand human behavior and, more specifically, the beliefs, perceptions, and motivations that guide decision-making and behavior.

Conceptually, the qualitative methodology assumes a dynamic and subjective reality through the data collection process. The researcher's role becomes critical as they interpret the results and the content of what is captured and how it is captured. One can only think of the interviewing process (a typical data collection technique for qualitative methodology) and how the interviewer can influence (consciously and unconsciously) the study due to their preconceptions and biases toward the investigated phenomenon. Because it concerns interactions among individuals (the researcher is included in some cases, like in an auto-biography), qualitative research is based on the constructivist epistemo-logical stance and heavily reflects the relativist ontological perspective. As such, it is heavily based on interpretation and induction.

The data analysis phase in qualitative methodology involves identi-fying persistent themes, categories, and relationships, cross-verification of the collected information from multiple sources of evidence (triangu-lation), cause-and-effect representations of the phenomenon under investigation, and testing the construct formulations with subsequent evidence. This process relies heavily on the researchers' rationality and healthy skepticism as they critically evaluate and verify their findings. Because of its heavy reliance on interpretation and small sample populations, the qualitative methodology has difficulty supporting the generalization of findings. Instead, the methodology ensures the trust-worthiness of results (usually through triangulation, member checking, etc.) and the results' transferability to similar social settings and research studies.

While the value of the qualitative methodology in getting to the bottom of issues and suggesting cause-and-effect relationships cannot be denied, there are criticisms concerning its rigor due to the "soft" nature of data (narratives) that are usually seen as limited (small samples) and subjective. Significant concerns are raised regarding the reliability, validity, and representativeness of the collected information, as frequently the methodology is judged in light of and according to quantitative research rules.

Mixed Methods

Qualitative and quantitative methods can be combined in various ways to form what is called mixed research methods (Harkiolakis, 2017). This is an attempt to draw from multiple epistemologies to frame and understand phenomena. As a result, researchers are supposed to increase their studies' validity (through triangulation) to reach generalizations that will support the formation of theories to describe the phenomena under investigation accurately. While combinations of methods seem to move away from the methodology and get closer to examining a research problem, many researchers view the methodology as a separate and independent epistemological approach to research, bringing mixed methods into the realm of pragmatism. Others, though, believe that paradigms are not seen as distinct but rather as overlapping or with fluid boundaries where one gives rise to and supports the other, so combining quantitative and qualitative methods is an acceptable way of conducting research.

In conclusion, choosing a methodology based on the data the researcher plans to collect is one guiding principle in developing a research design but not the only one. The researcher's epistemological and ontological stances play a crucial role in the type of methodology they choose, and one might go, for example, for a qualitative methodology (as in a case study of an organization) that includes the collection and processing of quantitative archival data (such as the balance sheets for a period of time). While research methodologies have solid philosophical roots, connecting philosophy and practice is essential as it provides the general strategy for making and processing observations. Because "practice" is a core ingredient of methodology, it means that the subject of inquiry/research has already been identified and considered in the chosen methodology. Here is where ontology and epistemology come into play. Our beliefs about reality and learning can influence our approach to inquiry and the way we observe the phenomenon under investigation.

3 The Role of Theory in Qualitative Research

Theory, theoretical frameworks, conceptual frameworks, and theory of method are 'terms that have blurred lines within qualitative methods literature and either suffer or benefit from widespread nuanced differences. In general, a theory is a big idea that organizes many other ideas with a high degree of explanatory power' (Collins & Stockton, 2018, p. 2). The theory of method (or methodology) guides on what method will help answer a research question. A conceptual framework best functions as a map of "concepts" that are defined in the extant literature and "frame" or "ground" a particular study. These concepts are grounded in a foundational theoretical framework that identifies the lens through which the study will interpret new knowledge.

Maxwell (2012) defined a conceptual framework as a tentative theory about the phenomena being studied that informs the whole of the study's design, noting that 'this may also be called the "theoretical framework" or "idea context" for the study' (p. 39). This use of theory in grounding a study's concepts helps the qualitative researcher refine goals, develop research questions, choose methodological approaches, identify potential threats to the trustworthiness of analyzed data, and define the research's significance. The primary source of the conceptual framework, from his perspective, does not necessarily need to be an existing theory. Four primary sources are options from which to derive a conceptual framework: (1) knowledge based on experience, (2) existing theory, (3) exploratory research, and (4) 'thought experiments' (p. 44).

The researcher's network or "frame" of concepts weaved from the literature are the guiding constructs of epistemology and theory for qualitative studies. Maxwell (2012) wrote that the conceptual framework includes 'the system of concepts, assumptions, expectations, beliefs, and theories that supports and informs your research' (p. 39). The author continues on the terms conceptual and theoretical:

DOI: 10.4324/9781003244936-3

I use the term in a broader sense, to refer to the actual ideas and beliefs that you hold about the phenomena studies, whether these are written down or not; this may also be called the "theoretical framework" or "idea context" for the study.

(p. 39)

Similarly, Merriam and Tisdell (2015) added:

Yet another point of confusion is that the terms *theoretical framework* and *conceptual framework* are often used interchangeably in the literature. We prefer *theoretical framework* because a theoretical framework seems a bit broader and includes terms, concepts, models, thoughts, and ideas as well as references to specific theories; further, conceptual frameworks are often found in the methodology chapter or section of a quantitative study wherein the concepts and how they are to be operationalized and *measured* are presented.

(p. 84)

A theory, according to Saldaña and Omasta (2018), encases research into a narrative about 'social life that holds transferable applications to other settings, context, populations, and possibly time periods' (p. 257). These 'big truths' have four properties: '(1) predicts and controls action through an if-then logic, (2) accounts for variation, (3) explains how and why something happens through causation, and (4) provides insights for improving social life' (Saldaña & Omasta, 2018, p. 257). Theory extension in case study research results from data collection and adds new knowledge to a conceptual framework that guides the study. Specific qualitative methodological approaches call for theory construction from a study's findings, such as grounded theory studies. Saldaña (2015) challenged the notion that theory construction should be the primary type of theoretical thought in qualitative research and urged researchers to consider utilizing noted theorists' frameworks to guide qualitative studies. Guba and Lincoln (1994) wrote that theory in qualitative research must be present within the guiding framework when searching out new knowledge, while Ridder (2017) specifically recommended using case study research for theory modification or extension.

Theoretical frameworks provide four dimensions of insight for qualitative research that include: (1) focus and organization to the study, (2) expose and obstruct meaning, (3) connect the study to existing scholarship and terms, and (4) identify strengths and weaknesses of the study (Maxwell, 2012). The theory makes it possible to highlight data and observations that another standing theory may misinterpret or overlook. Ineffective use of existing theories occurs, according to Maxwell, when researchers are not sufficiently critical of the theory or rely on it too much and when they make less than adequate use of it.

Merriam (2009) wrote that all research has a theoretical framework that is either explicit or implicit, even when utilizing an inductive approach, and she referred to a theoretical framework as the 'structure, scaffolding or frame' (p. 66) for the study. Merriam and Tisdell (2015) also included concepts, terms, definitions, and models in a theoretical framework. Consistent with Maxwell's assertion, Merriam (2009) wrote that all parts of a qualitative study are informed by a theoretical framework and described the relationship between the research problem and the conceptual framework as a 'set of interlocking frames' (p. 68).

The conceptual framework

> should show how [the writer] is studying a case in a larger phenomenon. By linking the specific research questions to the larger theoretical constructs or important policy issues, the writer shows that the particulars of this study serve to illuminate larger issues and therefore hold potential significance for that field.
>
> (Marshall & Rossman, 2011, p. 7)

Utilizing the literature to draw out parameters for the conceptual framework is an exercise marked by efforts targeting distinction and simplicity. Literature presenting the conceptual framework that shows how research and literature come together in molding a study is the most successful way to grant more in-depth knowledge on the particular contribution of extending or modifying a theory.

4   How Does the Novice Researcher Design a Multiple Case Study?

Case study design aligns with a research goal that can be met by answering phenomena-driven research questions and offers methods to extend a theoretical proposition. Yin (2017) recommended that the case study method is applicable when the research seeks to address an explanatory question, such as how or why something happened, or a descriptive question, such as what happened. Qualitative case studies are now an integral part of the business and management literature and are used by researchers to understand better actors and organizations' actions and outcomes in multiple fields (Klenke, 2016). Qualitative case studies generate holistic and contextual in-depth knowledge using multiple sources of data.

A case study is a "thick" or rich empirical description of a specific instantiation of a phenomenon, commonly with embedded (i.e., nested) levels of analysis and frequently relying on multiple data sources (Yin, 2017). A defining aspect of case study research is the researcher's *deep immersion* in the phenomenon. *Replication logic* is a second defining aspect—this refers to the fact that the researcher does not pool cases together and use pooled logic (i.e., combine cases) as in traditional theory-testing research; instead, the researcher analyzes each case as a stand-alone experiment. First, the researcher tries to understand the central research question within each case and then replicate these insights across each case. This analysis of one or more cases is done to detect patterns in the data that offer theoretical insights in constructs, theoretical relationships among those constructs, and sometimes propositions (Eisenhardt, 1989).

Three conditions that are useful in determining whether the case study design should be used as a research strategy have been articulated by Yin (2017). The first condition relates to the type of research question that is being considered. Case study research is most appropriate when the researcher is interested in "How," "What," and "Why" questions.

DOI: 10.4324/9781003244936-4

The second and third conditions relate to the extent of control over behavioral events and the degree of focus on contemporary events. Case study research is deemed appropriate when the researcher is interested in contemporary events and cannot control or manipulate behavioral events. Three case studies can be undertaken: descriptive case studies, exploratory case studies, and explanatory case studies (Yin, 2017). Case studies are particularly relevant when understanding complex social phenomena is needed because 'the case study method allows investigators to retain holistic and meaningful characteristics of real-life events' (Yin, 2017, p. 2). Additionally, case studies may be used in evaluation research to explain, describe, explore, or be used as a meta-evaluation.

Case studies may be undertaken for several reasons and are an appropriate approach when the researcher is interested in the process or seeks an in-depth understanding of a phenomenon because of its uniqueness. Stake (2005) identified three motivations for studying cases: intrinsic, instrumental, and collective. An intrinsic case study is undertaken because the case itself is of interest. An instrumental case study is undertaken to gain insight into an issue. The case becomes secondary because it facilitates an understanding of something else. A collective case study is undertaken when several cases are selected to provide insight into a phenomenon, population, or condition. A collective case study may result in an enhanced understanding of the phenomenon or theorizing.

Case studies can be descriptive, interpretative, or evaluative. Additionally, many qualitative case studies can be undertaken: ethnographic, historical, psychological, or sociological (Baxter & Jack, 2008). A recent, dynamic approach to case study design is that of the live case study, also utilized at Harvard Business School in recent years, from where the case study method for teaching has its origins (Neubert et al., 2020). Specifically, such live case studies function to immerse students in interactive working environments, so that system nuances and behavior can be observed in a way not possible through traditional methods (Neubert et al., 2020; Rapp & Ogilvie, 2019).

Academic work traditionally begins with a problem and establishes a literature base to substantiate the problem and record what researchers have said. Subsequently, it is possible and necessary to logically and visually organize the literature into a conceptual framework, demonstrating how it covers or leaves available room to explore specific questions. From this point on, the theoretical framework can represent a qualitative study's turning point or pinnacle. From the problem, we develop the research questions, which can provide data to address the problem. The research question in "gaps" is strongly related to existing theory, focusing on "How" and "Why" questions. The existing theory contains research gaps that point to assumed relationships that form a base for propositions and a framework that will match empirical data after being identified within the standing theory. This broad difference is even further pronounced using a design that targets the "social construction of reality."

The case study research design includes questions and interviews to uncover the participants' experiences, participant selection logic, data collection, field procedures, identified data analysis technique, and a template to report the multiple case study (Noor, 2008; Stake, 2013). Interviews are a primary source of data collection to answer a research question. Data triangulation is done in such a way as to limit problems related to constructing validity, given that multiple data sources offer different measures of a phenomenon. Several strategies can be used for data analysis (e.g., case description, investigating opposing explanations) and analytic techniques to compare proposed relationships with empirical patterns (Yin, 2017). Pattern-matching logic is employed to compare empirically and predicted patterns, supporting additional data analysis techniques (e.g., cross-case synthesis, time series analysis, explanation building, and logic models). Analytical generalization entails comparing the theory with the empirical results, which can be extended or modified (Ridder, 2017; Yin, 2017).

Designing a case study protocol allows researchers to augment their study's reliability (Baxter & Jack, 2008; Yin, 2017). The method and research design delineate the process of conducting a multiple case study (Tsang, 2013). A multiple case study's capacity to elicit common findings from different settings is one of its design strengths. In multiple case study research, theoretical replication involves testing a theory by comparing the findings with new cases. If pattern-matching between data and propositions emerges in a series of cases, theoretical replication can manifest through a new series of cases with contrasting propositions. The replication logic in case studies also allows developing a rich, theoretical framework (Nonthaleerak & Hendry, 2008; Yin, 2017).

Like cross-experimental designs, various authors (Yin, 2017) have stated that theoretical frameworks offer a base for generalization to new cases. By evaluating each case as a separate investigation in this study, replication logic can support generalizations. For multiple case studies, replicating logic has been likened to multiple experiments (Yin, 2012). Theories or hypotheses about the selected cases, essential for case study analysis and design, can be used to derive replication logic (Yin, 2012). The researcher applies further logic to develop consistent protocols for collecting data (Yin, 2012).

Ethical Concerns for the Case Study Researcher

Over the past century, ethics in research has become a primary concern for governing bodies and the public. Muhammad (2018) offers the case study research a detailed narrative on the history and contemporary ethical research principles of qualitative studies. During World War II, some scientific practices raised severe ethical concerns; thus, the Nuremberg Code was created during the Nuremberg War Crime Trials. This Code sought to establish ethical standards and practices in science; while science has dramatically benefited humanity, specific methodologies raised serious ethical questions (National Commission for the Protection of Human Subjects of Biomedical and Behavioral Research, 1978).

The Commission established three ethical principles to provide a framework from which scientific research and practice should be conducted: to distinguish practice and research; establish basic ethical principles; and methods by which the general principles should be applied (National Commission for the Protection of Human Subjects of Biomedical and Behavioral Research, 1978). Ethical guidelines were first established in 1978 by the U.S. Department of Health and Human Services as outlined in *The Belmont Report: Ethical Principles and Guidelines for the Protection of Human Subjects of Research.* The principles of respect for persons, beneficence, and justice are highlighted and serve to undergird ethical behavior.

Muhammad (2018) also wrote on the implications of the ethical principles for human research as described in *The Belmont Report.* The first ethical principle listed by the Commission is "respect for persons," a sentiment echoed by Yin (2017), who finds the dignified treatment of human beings to be of vital importance to a methodologically rigorous study. Respect for persons adheres to two fundamental assertions: that the individuality and competence of the participant must always be revered, and that not all individuals can deliberately apply self-reliance and governance. Therefore, all care was given to ensure respondents were not subject to external influence in responding to the research questions (Muhammad, 2018).

The second ethical principle of beneficence was developed to ensure the participant's well-being and that of society because of the research study. Researchers are culpable to ensure the benefits of the study outweigh reasonably anticipated risks that may occur during and after the study. By practicing beneficence, researchers actively guard research participants against physical and psychological harm. Finally, the third principle of justice requires fair and equitable treatment of all participants and a requirement that any study involving participants offers potential benefits to them.

The core of ethical qualitative research relies upon the safety and confidentiality of participants, in accord with the sensitivity of the topic and group; non-malfeasance relies upon honesty and discretion, and reasonable care must be exercised to maintain ethical standards. Researchers must consider efficacy, predisposition, and issues reflexivity when determining whether research is ethical. Researcher investigation of topics involving ethnicity requires transparency regarding the nature and purpose of the inquiry, diligence in protecting the confidentiality of the participants, and candor. Because the general nature of the multiple case study method involves the testimony of participants based on direct interaction or from observations, the responses often cannot be predicted or screened by the interviewer. Participants may share information in confidence, revealing very personal details of their life. Therefore, Muhammad (2018) wrote that it is imperative to explain to the participant the terms of research, including the purpose, terms of reciprocity, risk assessment analysis, terms of the agreement, and data access between the participant and researcher as well as any data collection sources used in the study, along with confidentiality, informed consent, and the ethical versus legal responsibilities that govern the study.

Researchers must embody integrity in all aspects of the research practice, exercising principles of good stewardship. Intellectual rights must be reported along with an accurate description of all contributions to the research project and forthrightness reporting potential and realized conflicts of interest compromising mutual adherence to responsibilities between researcher and participant (National Research Council, 2002). Finally, an ethical researcher takes action to remedy ethical concerns, matters of self-governance, forthrightness, dependability, and to maintain the participants' privacy and avoid a breach of trust. Participant empowerment, having participants honestly tell their experiences, remains a fundamental responsibility of case study researchers.

Anonymity may be necessary when dealing with sensitive or controversial topics; in case studies, it is necessary to determine if the identity of the case itself can be revealed while concealing the identity of the individual or whether the case and individuals can be identified without attributing specific identifiers (Yin, 2017). It is recognized that not all individuals or groups have the power of self-determination at their disposal; typically, human beings establish group-based hierarchical systems among themselves. Therefore, case study researchers should seek to give voice to the voiceless accurately.

Researchers must also avoid intrusion, refraining from soliciting private information unrelated to the current research topic. This is especially important in today's climate, where it is possible to obtain a great deal of personal information, available and sometimes voluntarily disclosed on the World Wide Web. Informed consent must now include a review of the "terms of use" of websites that may serve as instrumentation during the study and offer a comprehensive understanding to each participant of what is expected and what they may expect from the research project (Gelinas et al., 2017).

5 The Advantage of the Multiple Case Study Design for Management Researchers

The advantage of multiple case data analysis for leadership and management researchers is the ability to move from simple description to explanation of underlying organizational and behavioral dynamics that allows one to confirm, disconfirm, and extend theory that underlies the whole set of multiple cases (Mullen-Rhoads et al., 2018). Theory extension from case studies represents a vital research strategy (Bonett, 2012). It can contribute theoretical insights that are both rich and weighted on under-theorized phenomena and, as yet, inadequately explored. Entailing extensive immersion into a focal phenomenon, case research is appropriate for answering research questions regarding "How." The most successful research projects engender new theoretical insights related to "big picture" research questions that seek to fill significant gaps and dilemmas in theory. In multiple case research, after completing the within-case analyses, a researcher also does a cross-case analysis.

Comparing multiple cases makes it possible to "test" the theory emerging in each successive case using replication logic (Yin, 2017). Approaches used in comparing and contrasting cases (e.g., A to B, A to C, and B to C) compel the researcher to investigate and treat the data from more than one perspective and utilize various combinations. For example, relevant constructs can be identified by distinguishing differences and similarities across the cases. Measures of constructs can be summarized in tables (Miles et al., 2014). Researchers can use these construct tables as tools to advance insights that establish theoretical relationships among constructs.

Real-life phenomena can be scientifically studied in-depth and within the context of their environment using case study research. A person, a problem, an event, an organization, a group, and even an anomaly can be distinguished as a case (Ridder, 2017; Yin, 2017). In contrast to an experiment, a case's contextual conditions form part of the investigation. They are not controlled or outlined. No sample is seen to represent

DOI: 10.4324/9781003244936-5

a larger population. As such, case study research employs non-random sampling.

Contrary to quantitative logic, the case is selected precisely because it is of interest (Stake, 2005), or there may be theoretical reasons for selecting it (Eisenhardt & Graebner, 2007). Maximum variation (heterogeneity) sampling is used in qualitative sampling 'to document variations that have emerged in adapting to different conditions' (Lincoln & Guba, 1985, p. 200) and is the preferred sampling mode for constructivist inquiry (Lincoln & Guba, 1985). The multiple case study researcher can enact maximum variation sampling by purposefully selecting participants from a diverse set of organizational or geographical contexts.

In qualitative research, maximum variation sampling relies on the researcher's judgment to select participants with diverse characteristics to ensure maximum variability within the primary data. The multiple case study sample can be purposefully built up serially by using the criteria of including leaders and managers who would be information-rich for their study. This criterion-based sampling can gather a heterogeneous group of participants to support maximum variation sampling (Benoot et al., 2016). The sample size is determined by what the researcher wants to know, its purpose, and the sampling strategy and data saturation: 'The validity, meaningfulness, and insights generated from qualitative inquiry have more to do with the information-richness of the cases selected and the observation/analytical capabilities of the researcher than with sample size' (Patton, 1990, p. 185). Accordingly, the multiple case study researcher may collect data from individual participants representing their unit of analysis and conclude that a saturation point is reached since no new themes emerged from the data analysis.

To address a study's problem, the multiple case study design and the selection of the cases are categorized into two types: the *literal replication* and the *theoretical replication*. While the former means that case studies selected yield similar results, the latter means that case studies are selected to predict contradictory results. In a multiple case study, the "case" itself may be a person, event, entity, or another unit of analysis (Yin, 2017). Taking the example of a case as a person, a single case concerns one individual, whereas a multiple case study involves more than one person. This process aims to replicate the same results across multiple cases by exploring the differences and similarities between and within cases. The evidence resulting from the replication process is considered *robust* and *reliable* and can be utilized in extending theory from cases (Welch et al., 2020; Yin, 2017).

The contributions to theory extension of multiple case study research design lie in furthering in-depth knowledge dependent on context and identifying novel trends and new phenomena. Utilizing a multiple case study, the researcher can contribute new perspectives and construct new realities based on openness to new phenomena, the ability to avoid theoretical preconceptions, and opportunities to gain insights from collected data. Although Eisenhardt's (1989) multiple case study design is based on other philosophical assumptions and is used in various ways, a marked tendency remains to follow and quote her research strategy to advance new relationships and develop new constructs in real-life cases.

Incorporating Multiple Case Analyses in Research Methods

For academic and industry researchers, the multiple case study method provides ready access to several different examples, methods, problem-solving techniques, and bibliographic references that can be helpful when formulating study protocols, interview techniques, analytical methods, and exhibit or outcomes reporting. Researchers often provide one foundational case study example to illustrate key concepts and outcomes; however, utilizing multiple case study methods can illustrate how these different concepts can be seen in different situations, environments, markets, or experimental settings.

By showing such comparisons and contrasts, researchers can create linkages among cases—or show how they cannot be created—and use these to illustrate when best to use and to not use specific approaches and methods. For example, a scholar fielding a survey to both highly educated respondents and not very educated ones can demonstrate, through multiple case study writings, how different surveying methods worked (or did not work) based on specific segments of a larger survey pool. Future researchers can then use differentiated methods to create better stratified or segmented surveys to achieve better results more efficiently. By only looking at a single case study of such a survey, how to address such limitations across different survey segments may not be made as clearly.

In addition, researchers can add depth to bibliographic references and discover key points of agreement and disconnect by using multiple case study methods in their scholarship. This approach creates improved citations and references for future scholars and helps address a fundamental problem in case study-supported research: the "sample size of one" problem. When researchers use a single case study to buttress an analytical argument, provide qualitative justification for results, or demonstrate the use of a particular research method or paradigm, readers are often left with critical questions like: "But will this work in my case?" Alternatively, "Are these results generalizable to other situations/ industries/cases/firms?"

Thus, to help researchers use multiple case study methods, a few recommendations may prove helpful:

- **Utilize multiple case studies (at least three, if possible) to support key research outcomes**: Single cases can help researchers point out a key finding or two, but to create more impact, they should utilize more than two or three case studies if possible. This approach leads readers and other researchers to look for more than "sample sizes of one" when it comes to important hypotheses, methods, and findings.

- **While each case can stand alone, be sure to link them together with important research themes or "red threads"**: However, simply citing multiple cases is not sufficient if the researcher wishes to show generalizability of results. In addition to using multiple case studies, researchers should also link them together along key themes, foci, and outcomes to show important "red threads" to other readers. This will show not only connections among cases but also, again, get past the "sample size of one" challenge often associated with single case study works and articles.

- **Using separate bibliographies and references will help future researchers with method and outcome comparisons**: Each case should have its stand-alone bibliography and references. This will allow readers and other scholars to let cases "stand alone" if they wish to cite only a selected case(s) and avoid having to tease out which references belong to which cases individually. However, some researchers may end up duplicating references across case studies, but this is generally accepted in academic publications.

- **Utilizing exhibits that link multiple cases together works best**: Not only should researchers link case studies together along with key "red threads," as mentioned earlier, but they should also use an exhibit (or more) to connect cases, protagonists, methods, and outcomes visually. A good example of such graphical linkages is often seen in meta-analysis studies, where multiple studies are assessed simultaneously to determine broad concurrence across critical outcomes. A visual connection exhibit or "road map" is often helpful, especially for lay readers, to see how cases connect (or do not connect) to each other, and this technique also serves as a valuable checkpoint for authors to ensure that multiple case studies do make sense together as a package.

While this multiple case study approach for research design and writing creates more work for the author, such an approach will yield more compelling, generalizable results from scholarly efforts than just using a single case alone. Many readers and journal referees are wary of single case study examples because they look for outcomes and methods that have broader applicability across different situations, subject areas, and, in some cases, academic domains. However, writing such multiple case studies as part of research literature does take some practice, which is why utilizing coordinated (but separate) bibliographies and creating some visual/graphical "connection" exhibits are particularly beneficial.

6 Applying Data Collection Methods in Multiple Case Study Research

A fundamental element that influences methodology choice is the researcher's role and data collection methods for interpretation. The open-ended methods that are used in qualitative research are meant to explore participants' interpretations (usually collected in relatively close settings) and include, among others, interviewing, on-site observations, case studies, histories, biographies, ethnographies, and conversational and discourse analysis. Data and information are usually collected from samples of actors and their accounts of their perspectives and recollections of events and impressions they formed about specific situations they experienced. Because the case study method is grounded in the traditions of constructivist and relativist views, it is well suited for research that challenges established preconceptions of truth like male dominance and white supremacy. In a way, the method itself is a challenge to the traditional quantitative approaches that have dominated research for centuries.

By many, case study research is seen primarily as a discovery process, with explanatory potential that precedes quantitative research to prove its findings. The researcher starts with an interpretation of the phenomenon under investigation and proceeds to collect data (observations, interviews, etc.). Data collection methods widely used in case study research include interviews, focus groups, journaling, observational field notes, reflexive field notes, diaries, photovoice, archival data, social media mining, image-based methods, and text and web mining. As information is processed, the researcher reformulates the original interpretation, and after cycles of information collection, and interpretation, eventually develops a theory of what is observed. This process can be seen in interviews when a question might be followed with probes to clarify what the interviewee says and provide more depth. This cyclic aspect of the qualitative case study method makes it suitable for theory development, extension, or validation.

DOI: 10.4324/9781003244936-6

Interviews, observations, and documents are the primary means of collecting data in case study research. Concepts, themes, and relationships emerge from analyses within sites and across cases. Once emerged constructs have been identified, the researcher verifies in each case the relationships that emerge between the constructs. The logic supporting this approach is one of validation by replication. The researcher treats cases as experiments in which their hypotheses are replicated on a case-by-case basis. In replication logic, emergent relationships confirmed by cases improve confidence in their validity and theory extension by targeting the precision of constructs and emerging relationships.

Important themes and practical applications can be identified by collecting interview data using purposive sampling of 5–15 participants as a larger sample size can become an obstacle for an in-depth investigation (Merriam & Tisdell, 2015; Schram, 2006). The final sample size of a multiple case study is determined by data saturation (Eisenhardt, 1989). Triangulation, the method of integrating several data sources, strengthens a study's credibility by balancing each approach's strengths and weaknesses. Multiple data collection methods from multiple sources of evidence can be gathered to provide a study's research questions, such as interviews, reflective journaling, and analysis of archived data such as government reports and media reports on current leadership and management topics (Guion et al., 2011).

Collecting data can be particularly challenging for multiple case researchers. The sheer volume of data may overwhelm some novice researchers. Identifying patterns and themes among triangulated data can prove challenging for many researchers. However, the triangulated data is considered robust when researchers read, hear, and observe consistent data across multiple evidence sources. While there is no set rule, archival data are especially helpful in addressing the facts of a case regarding the associated who, what, where, and when. To address "How" and "Why" questions, interview and observation data are instrumental. To illustrate, a researcher can use blogs and news articles to understand which product innovations took place in an organization and the timeline they followed.

The researcher can gain insights through observations and interviews regarding processes and motivations related to such innovations. By combining archival and primary data, it is possible to build a more accurate account of the case in its entirety, one that includes insights into when, how, and why events took place the way they did. The data collection emphasizes archives, interviews, and (participant) observation (Flick, 2009; Mason, 2002).

As part of the data collection strategy, researchers employing the case study collect multiple data sources from triangulating results and providing a detailed case description (Eisenhardt, 1989; Ridder, 2016). The detailed description and analysis arising from a single case study can be used to enhance understanding of "how" and "why" things happen and thus represent the potential advantages of this type of research. Single case study research offers the chance to delve into a "black box" that presents itself and examines a phenomenon's deeper causes (Burns, 2000; Fiss, 2009). Data gathered and triangulated within a multiple case study design can help identify patterns and relationships and enable a researcher to test, extend, or create a theory (Gomm et al., 2000).

Guion et al. (2011) identified five approaches to triangulation commonly utilized in qualitative research. All may apply to supporting the trustworthiness of multiple case study results. Data triangulation, the most straightforward and most commonly used form of triangulation, utilizes different sources of data/information. Data is triangulated by looking for outcomes that are agreed upon by all "cases." The weight of evidence suggests that if every unit of analysis defines the issue from different points of view and results in an expected outcome, it is more than likely valid.

Investigator triangulation involves using several different investigators/evaluators in an evaluation project. Typically, this would manifest as an evaluation team that consists of your colleagues within your program area/field of study. In order to triangulate, each different evaluator would study the program using the same qualitative method (interview, observation, case study, or focus groups) to establish the validity of the findings. Theory triangulation involves the use of multiple professional perspectives to interpret a single set of data/information. Unlike investigator triangulation, this method typically entails using professionals outside of your field of study. One popular approach is to bring together people from different disciplines. However, individuals within disciplines are used if they are in different status positions. In theory, it is believed that individuals from different disciplines or positions bring different perspectives. Therefore, if each evaluator from the different disciplines interprets the information in the same way (draws the same conclusions), then validity is established.

Methodological triangulation involves the use of multiple qualitative and/or quantitative methods to study the program. If the conclusions from each of the methods are the same, then validity is established. In practice, this method may require more resources in order to evaluate the program using different methods. Likewise, it will require more time to analyze the data/information yielded by the different methods.

Finally, environmental triangulation involves using different locations, settings, and other critical factors related to the environment in which the study took place, such as time of the day, day of the week, or season of the year. The key is identifying which environmental factor, if any, may influence the information you received during the study. The environmental factor is changed to see if the findings are the same. If the findings remain the same under varying environmental conditions, the validity has been established.

To illustrate an example of how a multiple case study is designed to support a rigorous data collection process, let us examine how a qualitative multiple case study was developed by Sanders Muhammad and Halkias (2019), and which investigated the leadership experiences of African American women managers employed in predominantly black work environments. Aligning with this study purpose, the following central research question was developed by the researchers: *What are the leadership experiences of African American women managers employed in predominantly black work environments?* The central research question was designed after an exhaustive review of the extant literature to identify gaps in the experiences of African American women managers in a predominantly black work environment and whether, in this intra-racial workplace, this population pays an agentic penalty simply for being a woman in a leadership position (Livingston et al., 2012; Rosette et al., 2016). A literature gap was also identified on the career trajectory experiences of female managers in a same-minority workplace.

Sanders Muhammad and Halkias (2019) recruited using purposeful, criterion, and snowball sampling strategies and screened with the following inclusion criteria: adults over the age of 18; African American women managers; supervising primarily black employees for at least two years; and possessing in-depth knowledge about the topic of the study (Patton, 2014). Semi-structured interviews with a sample of ten African American women managers working in predominately black enterprises (Yin, 2017), reflective field notes, and literature examining experiences related to the purpose of the study (Merriam & Tisdell, 2015) were the sources of data used to explore the specific leadership experiences of African American women managers in a predominantly black work environment.

The study's interview guide consisted of standardized, open-ended questions on the leadership experiences of African American women. The interview protocol comprised four sections. The opening section consisted of pre-interview questions and socio-demographic characteristics (Hall, 2017), followed by instrumentation designed to reveal perceptions associated with skin tone within the participants'

7 The Data Analysis Process for Multiple Case Study Research

To thoroughly investigate a social phenomenon by comparing and contrasting differences between cases and considering each participant as an individual case, Yin (2017) suggested using a multiple case study. The situational complexities related to particular social settings are imperative to understanding the social and behavioral actions of the study sample as defined within the theoretical framework (Stake, 2013). In a multiple case study, the case itself may be a person, an event, an entity, or another unit of analysis. When focused on a person, a single case concerns one individual, where a study of more than one person constitutes a multiple case study.

Multiple cases may be conducted for several reasons: they extend emergent theory, fill theoretical categories, provide examples of polar types, or replicate previously selected cases to discover new theoretical directions (Bonett, 2012; Yin, 2017). In such a research design approach based on Yin's (2017) methodology and interpretation of the multiple case study, the case itself may be a person, and is often used in business and management studies in the scholarly literature, for example, Brown (2017) on airport managers, Howard et al. (2019) on women entrepreneurs, Komodromos (2014) on university employees, Neubert (2016) on tech firm owners, and Sanders Muhammad (2020) on African American women managers.

Cross-case synthesis is the technique recommended for data analysis to strengthen external validity and data trustworthiness and provide a more vigorous multiple case study research (Merriam & Tisdell, 2015). The analytic process includes both within-case and cross-case analyses (for multiple case study designs). In later stages of the analysis, related literature is often introduced to refine constructs and theoretical mechanisms. The rationale for adopting multiple case study research lies in the strength of replication logic (Yin, 2017). Concerning literal replication, cases are chosen to predict similar results. Regarding theoretical

DOI: 10.4324/9781003244936-7

replication, cases are chosen to predict results in contrast but based on theoretical reasons. Yin (2017) provided several recommendations that can be utilized to increase the multiple case study's reliability (protocol, database).

For the data analysis process, the case study researcher accumulates all the data collected from the interview transcripts, journaling notes, and archival data and develops categories and themes through content analysis (Merriam & Tisdell, 2015). To ensure accurate data, transcription of data can be used for the analysis and then analyzed, coded, and categorized using a Microsoft Excel spreadsheet (Yin, 2017). With the formation of a case study database, the identification of themes, words of significance, viewpoints, and documented work are analyzed and organized through thematic analysis to assist with developing themes and models from the data (Yin, 2017).

Data analysis when conducting a multiple case study includes two stages. The first stage involves a within-case analysis of each of the selected cases in learning about the contextual variables, and the second stage consists of a cross-case analysis of data to find similarities and differences across the categories and themes (Yin, 2017). Regarding the within-case analysis, the data collection of transcribed interviews and field notes from each case is arranged in data segments, indexed with line numbers, and arranged in line with the interview questions for ease of identifying code.

Using a Microsoft Word table, the identified codes are recorded in a matrix form with columns that capture the data segments, the assigned codes, and the researcher's reflective notes (Saldaña, 2015). As the researcher creates memos, the goal is to describe the emerging patterns and categories and other topics of reflection. The codes are classified with shared common meaning into categories, then progressing into themes. In the cross-case analysis, each case is evaluated separately before synthesizing the data from each case, strengthening the study's results (Eisenhardt & Graebner, 2007; Yin, 2017).

The descriptive coding strategy analyzes the raw data collected to assign meaning to the data segment (Saldaña, 2015). Using the descriptive coding strategy allows for the emergence of words and phrases for further categorization and thematic analysis. The in-depth experiences of participants are captured from the raw data (transcripts) of their interviews. Data saturation occurs during the data analysis process. Yin's (2017) recommendation is for the case study researcher to follow a *ground-up* strategy to analyze the data that allows critical concepts to emerge by carefully examining the data. This strategy is the most suitable method to explore the data for insights and relationships to align the emerging concepts with the research question (Yin, 2017). The ground-up strategy is consistent with the descriptive coding method (Saldaña, 2015).

In qualitative data analysis, the objective of coding does not involve the calculation or tally of an object; it is "fracturing" data by rearranging text descriptions to compare items within the same category (Maxwell, 2012). Saldaña (2015) recommended that the descriptive coding method is suitable for novice qualitative researchers who are still learning how to code qualitative data. The words and phrases of segmented data can share the same meaning with assigned codes, while the categories are a way to connect them (Maxwell, 2012). The descriptive coding method is applied as the primary analytical technique in the multiple case study, consisting of assigning symbolic meanings to data segments and providing a collection of words or phrases for indexing and categorizing data (Saldaña, 2015).

The coding process is a primary method for analyzing qualitative, exploratory research studies (Saldaña, 2015). A standardized, systematic approach when collecting and analyzing data ensures an effective coding process. By aligning the data collection and analysis, it offers concurrent, useful emergence of key concepts and understanding the research problem (Stake, 2013). The method involves manual coding, categorization, and recognition of emergent patterns and themes across the cases. After coding the data from the interview questions, the aim is to link the themes to classifications grounded in the scholarly literature. The researcher identifies codes of common themes that arise from the participants' interview responses while collecting research and other field notes (Merriam & Tisdell, 2015).

Cross-case synthesis allows researchers to determine if the case studies are comparable by analyzing the collected data's convergence and divergence (Yin, 2017). In the process, data segments are identified from transcripts, and codes are recorded to capture emerging patterns (Saldaña, 2015). The same coding method analyzes the data within and across cases (Yin, 2017). When the same coding method is used to analyze the data within and across the cases, it allows for replicating cases, comparing and contrasting results for an in-depth understanding of the phenomenon under study (Yin, 2017). We suggest that novice researchers select the descriptive manual coding method described by Saldaña (2015) to analyze the data rather than use Computer Assisted Qualitative Data Analysis (CAQDAS) programs. Keep in mind that no software program can engage with the data as much as the researcher. Using the manual descriptive coding method, the researcher can become deeply involved in the data, as is the traditional purpose of the data analysis.

Thematic analysis is used in the descriptive coding method to code the data systematically (Saldaña, 2015). The systematic process for mapping the structure of common themes allows the researcher to shift from collecting to analyzing the data (Saldaña, 2015). The case study researcher may discover data segments from the participants' transcripts describing experiences and categorize keywords through an indexing method. A Microsoft Excel spreadsheet may be used for the manual coding process. After checking the participants' transcribed responses, the interview notes are entered into the spreadsheet.

During data analysis, the case study researcher analyzes the participants' responses by finding patterns while reviewing and incorporating the differences across data sources for triangulation (Merriam & Grenier, 2019). The Microsoft spreadsheet may include data segments, categories, and themes based on the interview discussions and the transcribed responses. The process involves the researcher recognizing and differentiating the patterns emerging from the themes and disregarding the nonrecurring evidence attributed to individual case compositions.

Using the ground-up strategy recommended by Yin (2017), the case study researcher can identify raw data codes and offer critical concepts to emerge by examining data by obtaining the relevant phrases from the transcribed responses and assigning them with codes for further analysis. With this coding process, emerging themes can be categorized from each participant's interview and common relationships across the participants' interviews (Yin, 2017). Through triangulation of data and word coding, a broader detection of patterns emerges and increases the study's dependability, drawing attention to common relationships across multiple cases (Yin, 2017). Identifying coding categories and their deriving themes facilitates the objective answering of a study's central research question.

The cross-case synthesis involves comparing and contrasting cases rather than just analyzing individual cases for content analysis (Halkias & Neubert, 2020; Yin, 2017). The cross-case synthesis technique is a method that handles each case separately while accumulating the findings across a series of individual cases. Consequently, the cross-case synthesis is not different from other research syntheses that aggregate and compare findings across a series of individual studies. The research designs with both within-case and cross-case synthesis have proven to offer a more consistent platform to generate theoretical propositions and constructs than designs that use only the within-case analysis.

To illustrate the cross-case synthesis method, let us review the data analysis procedures used by Shepherd (2020) in a multiple case study with the purpose of in-depth understanding of business intelligence (BI) experts' views of the critical success factors (CSFs) needed for self-service BI initiatives among casual users in the post-implementation stage. Shepherd (2020) used multiple data sources to offer such an understanding. Archival data were added to journaling/reflective notes in support of the researcher's role. As the researcher read the notes, she strived for objective interpretations aligned with the research problem and purpose. The research was an iterative verification process between collecting and analyzing data to answer the research question (Shepherd, 2020). The emerging patterns and related categories and themes helped deepen the understanding of the study participants' responses within each interview and across interviews. Repeating categories and themes that emerged during the iterative process signaled that no further coding was necessary to obtain new information.

Shepherd (2020) constructed a hierarchal coding frame to organize codes and themes based on how they relate to one another, as is shown below. Five coding categories based on the conceptual framework emerged from three root nodes, and 15 themes were gleaned from the thematic analysis of the coding categories. Below is an example of the first and last thematic analysis hierarchies (of five total) where Shepherd (2020) presents her multiple case study data analysis.

The **first root node** was the *skill characteristics of casual users* that included **one code category**, effective BI skills for the casual user with the following **two themes**: (a) self-reliance and (b) understanding the multidimensional analysis concept.

The **final root node** was *defining the CSFs among casual users in the post-implementation stage for a successful competitive performance* that included the **coding category** of the CSFs for BI systems implementation with the following **five themes**: (a) continuous training, (b) user satisfaction with participation, (c) casual users belong to the business team culture, (d) responsive managerial support, and (e) effective organizational communication systems.

Shepherd (2020) conducted a comprehensive data analysis, namely within-case and cross-case data analysis, that included merging data for analysis from multiple data sources: the semi-structured interview protocol, archival data in the form of business reports, industry reports, and media articles on BI, and journaling/reflective field notes. Once a case study researcher is done with the data analysis and triangulation of data from multiple sources, it is time to evaluate and present the quality criteria for the *trustworthiness* of their study results. Proving the trustworthiness of multiple case study results is essential if those results are utilized to support the extension of the theory grounding the study.

Quality Criteria Building the Trustworthiness of Multiple Case Study Results

As qualitative research is inherently subjective, qualitative researchers need to use a combination of different methods to ensure and sustain the trustworthiness of their multiple case studies. This section will discuss four quality criteria of trustworthiness as recommended by seminal qualitative methodologists Lincoln and Guba (1986), the preferred methods, and our recommendations to strengthen the trustworthiness of a multiple case study. In Table 7.1, the quality criteria for trustworthiness issues are credibility, transferability, dependability, and confirmability, which are listed with their quantitative criteria counterparts: internal validity, external validity, reliability, and objectivity.

An essential method to ensure the *credibility* of a multiple case study is *member checking* (Lincoln & Guba, 1986). Research participants review the transcript of their interview to confirm the accuracy of

Table 7.1 Definition of Criteria of Trustworthiness

Quality criteria	Quantitative counterpart	Definition
Credibility	Internal validity	*Credibility* defines the extent to which the researcher is confident in the research findings based on the collected data.
Transferability	External validity	*Transferability* explains the degree to which the research findings can be transferred or replicated to other contexts, cases, and situations.
Dependability	Reliability	*Dependability* relates to the accuracy and consistency of the data collection, analysis, and theme development process of a multiple case study research project.
Confirmability	Objectivity	*Confirmability* is the degree to which other researchers can confirm the research findings. It intends to ensure the research findings were derived from the data collected and are not influenced by researcher biases.

Table 7.2 Methods to Strengthen the Trustworthiness of Qualitative Case Study Results

Criteria	Method
Credibility	Member checking Triangulation Saturation and sampling method Alignment Peer review (or participation of multiple researchers, interviewers, data analysts, and debriefings with supervisor) Iterative or probing questioning Negative case analysis Pilot study
Transferability	Detailed documentation and thick description Variation of sampling and data collection methods
Dependability	Detailed documentation and thick description External audits Triangulation
Confirmability	Reflexivity Audit trail Data coding

the data. Member checks may also include questions about emerging patterns to better understand contextual meanings of the interviewee's specific terms and help reduce the impact of researcher bias.

In Table 7.2, we mention additional methods to strengthen the credibility of a multiple case study. *Triangulation* describes using different sources of evidence like interviews, observations, and case study documents to benefit from the advantages of the different data collection methods and to cross-check statements and facts (Yin, 2017). *Saturation, sample size, and sampling method*s are also essential methods to ensure credibility. There is a trend toward using higher sample sizes in multiple case study research. Often, researchers may achieve saturation with relatively small sample sizes of 15–20 research participants.

Sample sizes in qualitative studies are often based on the relatively homogenous inclusion criteria, identical contexts, or geographic proximity with similar perspectives on the phenomenon. Using criterion-based sampling may help the researcher to gather a heterogeneous group of participants to support maximum variation sampling and theory extension with multiple case study results. Maximum variation sampling in qualitative research relies on the researcher's judgment to select participants with diverse characteristics to maximize variability within the primary data.

Baškarada and Koronios (2017) described *transferability* as the extent to which the study results can be transferred to similar situations and contexts. Yawar and Seuring (2017) referred to transferability as external validity, the ability to use the research findings in another setting different from the research study itself. Yin (2017) stated that when the study results have meaning to others who are not part of this research project, then the qualitative research has fulfilled the transferability criterion. *Detailed documentation and thick description* about the sample, the setting, the boundaries, and the outcomes of the study allow other researchers to replicate it (Marshall & Rossman, 2016; Yin, 2017). *Variation of data collection and sampling methods* to recruit subject matter experts with different perspectives on the research phenomenon under investigation improves the credibility and transferability of research findings.

Dependability relates to the accuracy and consistency of the data collection, data analysis, and theme development process of a multiple case study research project (see Table 7.1). When the research findings are consistent and repeatable, the research is dependable (Lincoln & Guba, 1986). The primary method to ensure dependability is detailed documentation of the research process to allow other researchers to replicate the study. Other methods include external audits to review the research documentation and triangulation. As dependability is closely related to credibility, the same methods can be used (Lincoln & Guba, 1986).

Confirmability is the degree to which the results of an inquiry could be confirmed or collaborated by other researchers about one's data (Anney, 2014). The most important method to ensure *confirmability* is *reflexivity*. Reflexivity is about acknowledging your role in the research, that you are part of the research process, and that your prior experiences, assumptions, and beliefs may influence the research process. Confirmability is reached when the results of an inquiry are neutral, accurate, as unbiased as possible, and free of *reflexivity* or the researcher's expressions of inner thoughts, feelings, and insights. Researchers document the relationship between themselves and the research participants and the context of their interviews. Proven tools to ensure reflexivity are *data coding* and *audit trails*.

Qualitative methodology processes such as triangulation, a purposely selected variant sample, and audit trails that capture the researcher's background, context, and prior understanding are useful in developing a 'commonality of assertion' (Stake, 2013). In his study on change management in the healthcare industry, Selsor (2020) kept a collection of reflective field notes and journaling throughout his multiple case study process to capture his own beliefs and observational interpretations. Reflective field notes are written observations recorded during or immediately following participant observation and are considered critical to understanding phenomena encountered during the study process. Additionally, documents such as written notes, reports, and materials from the environment, including pictures, videos, and pamphlets, were used by Selsor (2020) to become more immersed in the environment of his multiple case study participants. Selsor's (2020) reflective field notes helped reduce his biases by increasing self-awareness before, during, and after the data collection process and during data analysis.

Our shortlist of recommendations for qualitative researchers to ensure the trustworthiness of their multiple case studies begins with alignment, followed by triangulation (data sources and sampling) and detailed documentation of the whole research project, including data, findings, and reflective field notes. We recommend using different sampling methods to recruit participants from different backgrounds with diverging experiences and perspectives on the research topic. Creating *alignment* between the main parts (problem statement, purpose, research question and methodology, conceptual framework, research findings) of a multiple case study is an essential driver of research quality and helps develop a transparent chain of evidence. *Peer review* (or the participation of multiple researchers, interviewers, data analysts in the research project, and debriefings with superiors) is another method to strengthen the credibility of a multiple case study. It will help researchers identify their preferences and biases. Other methods to ensure and sustain credibility are *iterative and probing questioning* to uncover inconsistencies in the answers of the research participants, *pilot study*, or a *negative case analysis* (Miles et al., 2019).

8 Extending Theory with Multiple Case Study Design

Theory extension achieved through a multiple case study design rests on three methodological pillars: a data analysis process of rich and comprehensive data, an influential research design, and a well-developed research question that directly aligns with the study's purpose. Each conceptual construct is grounded in well-measured and appropriate data from the literature. Rigorous multiple case study designs control for theoretical variation and help establish transferability and generalizability (Stake, 2010). A thorough literature review must be presented to identify new and unanswered questions and refine theoretical contributions after the study. Through a two-step process, evaluation of multiple data sources through a triangulation process is performed to determine the credibility of the evidence of the phenomena. In essence, the data is first analyzed using thematic analysis and then further evaluated with a cross-case synthesis method (Yin, 2017).

The multiple case study design can produce detailed descriptions and cross-case analyses of leadership and management phenomena using constructs to compare the collected qualitative data to earlier literature. Yin (2017) emphasized that multiple cases strengthen study results through replication logic, thus increasing the findings' robustness. The multiple case study researcher may choose to use literal replication (where cases corroborate each other) or theoretical replication (where the cases cover different theoretical conditions) to establish replication logic. Since case studies rely on analytical rather than statistical generalizations, replication logic provides external validation to the findings. Each case can serve to confirm or disconfirm the conclusions drawn from the others.

The term multi-site case study is often used in the same sense as comparative case studies, multiple case studies, and the term "collective case studies" used by Robert Stake. Used to examine a current and defined phenomenon common to two or more naturalistic or real-world settings,

DOI: 10.4324/9781003244936-8

a multi-site case study provides opportunities to understand an event, individual, group, program, or policy through multiple representations of the phenomenon under study. That is to say, a more comprehensive understanding of a phenomenon can emerge by shedding light on the implications, experiences, and effects of a phenomenon in multiple settings. In such a study, the research design is usually the same across all the sites, meaning the researcher studies the same phenomenon or unit(s) of analysis in the context of the same key research questions. Further, the researcher employs the same or similar approaches to collecting, analyzing, and reporting data across all the sites. A multi-site case study can enable valid replication claims and cross-site syntheses in addition to producing site-specific findings.

A variation of the single case study, a multiple case study entails more than one observation of a phenomenon; this makes replication possible, using multiple cases to independently confirm emerging constructs and propositions. Further, it enables theory extension and cases to bring out a phenomenon's complementary aspects. This process results in a theory that is more robust, generalizable, and developed. As opposed to research using multiple cases, single case research may reveal fascinating stories, but it is not as likely to support a high-quality theory. Multiple case studies begin with data and end with theory building, construction, or extension. Given that deductive research reverses operations' order, it stands to reason that the two are not that different. The similarities include a designated population that observations are drawn from, an a priori-defined research question and definition of constructs and, where possible, their measurement with triangulated data.

A multiple case study design aligns with social phenomena to be explored and develops an appropriate case study to address the research problem's nature (Yin, 2017). Since multiple case studies are based in natural settings with the intent of understanding the process of an under-examined area, a holistic understanding of the phenomenon can thus be explored (Eisenhardt, 1989; Stake, 2013). This method enables the researcher to explore differences within and between cases. Yin (2017) argued that the multiple case study design is relevant for replication and allows researchers to address a complex social phenomenon relevant when comparing different studies.

Case study designs help examine events when behaviors cannot be manipulated and seek a greater understanding of an issue. A multiple case study investigating a social phenomenon can involve individuals living within a social context as a separate unit of analysis (Yin, 2017). When the data focus is only on individuals in a multiple case study design, the study's central phenomenon is the context and not the study's target. The unit of analysis in a multiple case study can be a person, place, organization, or event, and as such, this design allows for investigating differences within and between cases.

A multiple case study design aims to replicate findings across cases and allow the researcher to link the research question and the research conclusion. Because comparisons are drawn, cases are chosen carefully so that the researcher can predict similar results across cases or predict contrasting results based on the conceptual framework (Yin, 2017). Comparing and contrasting results between multiple cases lead to more robust outcomes when using inductive theory. For any such outcomes to be persuasive, utilizing a specific research method and design has to rely on arguments rooted in the methodological literature (Eisenhardt & Graebner, 2007).

Qualitative researchers use multiple cases to arrive at both theoretical and actionable insights. A multiple case study allows the researcher to investigate a social phenomenon, comparing and contrasting cases in the same social context while contemplating each participant as a separate entity (Yin, 2017). The situational complexities associated with specific social contexts are vital to understanding social and behavioral interaction variables within a more extensive system (Stake, 2013). Yin (2017) suggests the qualitative method for probing questions, contributing originality, using various data sources. Eisenhardt and Graebner (2007) recommended that researchers utilize the multiple case study approach that includes more than one case when the study's goal is to make an original contribution to a theoretical or conceptual framework and provide a rich, compelling picture of human interaction as compared to a single case study.

There are numerous ways to analyze the data within multiple case studies. The researcher's ontological, epistemological, and other methodological stances will inevitably influence the analytic approach selected. Ideally, a researcher's view of what constitutes "reality" and how meaning comes from knowing are explicitly acknowledged, underpinning features of a multi-site case study. The approach used to analyze a descriptive case will likely be different from those used in exploratory or explanatory multi-site case studies. When the design, conduct, analysis, and reporting of a multiple case study are sound, the findings may be more compelling than those from a sound study where the sample is one cohort or a single phenomenon.

9 Incorporating Multiple Case Design and Methodologies into Teaching and Professional Practice

Until now, the text has focused on how to design and write multi-case study outputs. Careful attention has been given to show readers how these multiple case studies relate to basic (qualitative) research methodologies, including data collection, analysis, and presentation. In addition, readers will note how the multiple case study design and writing approaches extend existing case study frameworks to support discovery, learning, and pedagogy in various academic and non-academic/practitioner contexts.

However, a process for integrating such multi-case study designs and outputs into existing curricula and research, for teachers and researchers, or into current practice and advisory work for consultants and other (business) practitioners is needed. In this chapter, such frameworks and processes for how academic instructors, researchers, and industry practitioners can inculcate such multiple case study methods into their teaching, research, and practice, respectively, will be discussed. However, the authors acknowledge that in many cases, the lines among teaching, research, and practice applications are often blurred at best; thus, some crossover or blended uses of these tools are expected and encouraged.

For Faculty: Integrating Multi-Case Methods in Existing Curricula

Faculty in business and law disciplines, for example, are quite accustomed to teaching case studies using what is generally accepted as the "case method." Students are assigned cases to read in advance, usually with some guiding questions to address, and then come together individually or in groups to "solve" the case (or the assigned questions of interest) in a group setting with the instructor present and guiding the discussion and debate. Faculty usually assign a case to accompany a specific topic area of discussion in the course syllabus; for example, one might assign

DOI: 10.4324/9781003244936-9

a case focused on new market entry when discussing the broader strategic management concepts of competition and differentiation. Cases are usually assigned to be read or "solved" before the instructor's lecture on the particular topic; however, using cases to reinforce prior lecture material is also common.

By reading the assigned case, students will get a "real-world" feel for the material. While students might not yet know what competition or differentiation means in a strategy context, they will "see" it in the case materials. Alternatively, if such concepts have already been covered in a lecture in a more "academic" sense, then students will see real-world examples of such concepts in a case assignment that follows a lecture. Many forums and advisory writings have proffered approaches and techniques for instructors to use in order to teach effectively—and, indeed, to "choreograph," as some point out—case studies (see notes from Harvard Business Publishing on December 16, 2020, "How to Teach Any Case Online. Become the 'Author' of Each Case Study you Use in Your Virtual Classroom", and on April 13, 2021, "The Art of the Case Method. Part 3: Exploring the Instructor's Choreographic Role in Case-Method Teaching").

While many of these best practices are helpful for faculty, they tend to focus only on specific types of cases and their teaching methods. In general, most case studies in extant business school curricula, for example, tend to focus on "singular" dimensions; that is, they focus on a single problem, usually for a single market player or individual (case protagonist) at a single point in time. For example, a new leader in an organization may face a particular problem motivating other leaders/managers to change strategic direction, or a firm may face choices around market entry for a specific product or service vis-à-vis a fixed set of competitors.

Of course, the use of such "single-threaded" cases is widely apparent, as are the teaching methods. However, adopting these methodologies to multiple case study materials is rarely seen in top business school programs worldwide. Thus, how can multiple case study instructional materials be used in (existing) course pedagogy once designed? Since most case studies are designed for coverage during a one-course lecture or meeting period, how can multiple case study materials be utilized in single-lecture contexts or across multiple instructional periods? How can assignments be structured so that students receive maximum learning benefits from multiple case study materials while still meeting key learning objectives for a course?

Faculty and instructors may find the following suggestions helpful when addressing some of the questions just posed:

- **Use multiple case studies to drive comparisons and contrasts of different lecture concepts**: Single case study approaches allow instructors to explore some details of case facts and situations; however, using multiple cases allows for more comparative learning. For example, in a single case study, students may reflect on the pros and cons of a particular approach or technique in the case. However, students and instructors compare and contrast differing approaches to the same underlying lecture content, problem, or situational discussion in a multiple case study setting. For example, if one firm chooses to improve profits with revenue-increasing efforts while another chooses to reduce costs, such comparisons of different techniques and strategies can be explored further. Such comparisons and contrasts in single case studies are often left as a thought exercise or as a series of "What if" questions and considerations that may be hard for some students to conceptualize without a concrete (alternative) example.
- **Try replacing just one case with multiple case study content**: When implementing this novel multiple case study approach, faculty should replace just one case with a multiple case study package. In this way, instructors will see how such a case method works differently (and perhaps better) when compared to a traditional case study. Making wholesale changes to courses and curricula is not recommended at first. However, with more learning and familiarity with multi-case writing and teaching, some faculty may choose to create a blend of single-subject case studies and multiple case study packages in a course/curriculum.
- **Allow a multiple case study analysis to span more than one lecture or class period**: A case assignment takes up one class period or lecture session for many instructors and students. While this allows instructors to cover more (independent) case studies in courses, this approach often leaves some case questions and pedagogy unexplored and not discussed in as much detail if more time were permitted. Instead, use multiple case studies to broaden and deepen the conversations (and assignments) around differing approaches, methods, and techniques of case protagonists. While this may take more than one teaching session, connecting multiple such cases over more than one session may prove more effective than attempting to teach multiple independent/disconnected cases across multiple sessions.
- **Use the interstitial periods between lectures/class periods for additional "depth" assignments and reflections**: If faculty decide to let multiple case study materials span multiple lecture/class periods,

they can also create intermediate/interstitial assignments that draw connections among multiple cases (and instructional topics). These assignments can build on each other, too; for example, a first assignment can ask students to comment on, say, the pros and cons of a particular approach from one case study. Then, after this case study has been discussed, an additional assignment can be given that asks students to compare/contrast methods of another case protagonist with those from the first case addressed. In addition, or instead, instructors can ask students to provide their reflection— or even assignment "do-overs" after an initial session of multiple case coverage—so students see how additional case coverage and instruction inform better and improved thinking.

- **Structure assignments that build on prior ones (and possibly foreshadow ones to come)**: In addition to using intermediate assignments to build on prior ones, faculty can also choose to utilize "foreshadowing" assignments; that is, an assignment that asks students to read ahead in the multiple case collection and to consider some of the same (or different) assignment topics put forth with a prior assignment. In this way, students can be asked if their "solutions" to earlier assignments still apply to future parts of the multiple case study under consideration. This prevents "one size fits all" solution thinking and forces students to create customized solutions that "adapt" to the case situation in question even though the overarching lecture content and foci are preserved across case studies. For example, a faculty member can discuss how a higher court interprets a legislative statute in general but can then drill down to different local contexts, for example, to see how local jurisdictions enforce such legislation using multiple case study techniques. In these ways, such differences can be compared and contrasted using real data/examples instead of "What if" scenarios/ hypotheses.
- **Be sure to tie all case readings and assignments back to key course learning objectives (essential for accreditation reviews)**: Finally, faculty should make sure to directly tie any/all multiple case study materials back to original/source course learning objectives. Learning objectives should not change for courses, necessarily; however, how they are achieved using multiple case methods versus single case ones should be noted. Such improvements should garner praise from accreditors since multiple case studies are a bit more complex to develop, field, and teach; however, the student achievement and accomplishment of learning objectives will be done such that comparisons and contrasts of lecture concepts are

enforced, students learn that not all problems or cases can be solved in one class period, solutions to new/later problems often build on solutions from prior problems, and reflections on students' learning is a valuable assignment component as well.

Of course, such multiple case study approaches are not without their downsides or critics. Some critics claim that such multiple case studies either "dilute" focus on specific single case concepts or create more confusion than clarity in students' minds since the same learning concepts may apply differently in different parts of multiple case study packages. Multiple case methods also require a bit more instructor overhead and classroom choreography. However, when placed against the student learning and faculty teaching advantages, the multiple case study method allows for deeper and broader content coverage, improved student–student and student–instructor dialog, and more connectedness through assignments and other course pedagogy.

For Practitioners: Utilizing Multi-Case Designs in Advisory and Training Engagements

Finally, we consider the utility of the multiple case study approach in the practitioner world—particularly those in the professional services, advisory, consulting, and training/executive education domains. The use of such multiple case studies in training and executive education can be modeled after the suggestions proffered in the "For Faculty" section above. For example, using multiple examples of successful and unsuccessful negotiation strategies across different topics, industries, situations, and participants is often seen in corporate or executive education contexts in a course focused on trust-building and negotiation success. Thus, the focus will be on how professional advisors and consultants can utilize multiple case study methods in their daily client duties.

In most consultative situations, advisors determine root causes of challenges posed by clients, conduct analyses to determine solutions/ options, and then propose recommendations, often with action or implementation plans, to help clients implement policy, operational, strategic, or organizational changes that will address the underlying challenges. As part of this problem framing and problem-solving process, clients often ask their advisors to provide examples of similar problems, solutions (with pros and cons), and corrective actions that other similar individuals, organizations, or industries have implemented successfully or unsuccessfully. These exemplars provide clients with some background and baseline information from which to accept or reject/modify proposals put forth by consultants and advisors. (Whether these advisors or consultants are inside or outside the organization under study is insignificant; here, the multiple case study design may just as easily be used by outside consultants.) Thus, providing multiple case studies as evidence to support analyses, findings, and recommendations is essential for practitioners.

To utilize the value of multiple case studies, practitioners should consider the following practices:

- **Utilize cases from similar and different situations to offer validation for customized analyses and recommendations**: The best uses of multiple case study methods in practice comprise both similar and different background situations—various "theories of the case"—so clients and analysis recipients can see not only situations like theirs but also different ones where similar analyses and solutions may apply. This allows advisors to provide a more comprehensive array of examples where their proposed analyses and solutions have been implemented and thus add more credibility to their recommendations.
- **Acknowledge differences in both recommendations and outcomes where appropriate**: Not all multiple case study documentation should necessarily completely align with a consultant's proposed solutions and next steps. In fact, good learnings and value-added from advisors often come from demonstrating different analyses and outcomes from alternative recommendations. This allows clients to see broader contexts in which a consultant's analyses and recommendations reside and show how the same recommendations can sometimes lead to different outcomes for different situations and clients. By showing clients a broader "universe" of possible recommendations and solutions, consultants can prove that they are not providing "one size fits all" solutions or "cookie-cutter" recommendations to clients.
- **Note special circumstances from past case studies and current situations that may warrant extra attention**: Every situation and solution is different, so advisors should note any special considerations—market forces, economics, political environments, legal or technical constraints, etc.—that may shape specific analyses for or outcomes from a specific case study in a multiple case study collection. While these special circumstances may or may not apply to the specific client situation at hand, advisors should be well-versed in these specific circumstances of multiple cases in order to fairly represent them to recipients of recommendations.

- **Offer counterfactual case examples to balance all recommendations and next steps**: In addition to case examples that support an advisor's conclusions, consultants should also provide counterexamples if possible to demonstrate a depth of analysis. By showing case examples where specific recommendations or analyses may not have been appropriate, advisors can narrow in on why such advice may be appropriate for the specific client situation.
- **Graphics should accompany any prose**: As mentioned when discussing faculty and researcher application of multiple case study tools, advisors would be well-served to offer graphical linkages among multiple case studies when supporting their recommendations and next steps. These connection mappings will help clients see similarities and differences between multiple case studies put forward for consideration vis-à-vis their situations and environments in which they have sought help.

Essential connections among supporting case studies, advisors, and practitioners can utilize these multiple case study collections to support their recommendations while also showing "what ifs" that should be considered as implementation plans are developed. This chapter discussed several approaches and methods that faculty, researchers, and practitioners can employ when utilizing multiple case study methods in their courses, classrooms, research bibliographies, and on-the-job writing and training materials. By preparing and connecting such multiple studies—both in prose and visually via case connections graphics or exhibits—all creators can provide more value to their students, scholarly colleagues, and clients than would be possible with single case studies alone.

10 Writing and Publishing Multiple Case Study Research

The multiple case study design in a dominantly qualitative paradigm can explore and understand the management and leadership process in novel and meaningful ways. The multiple case study design utilized to study individual leaders and managers or multiple groups and organizations can be developed to provide rich and detailed data regarding the context of leadership behaviors and managerial competencies. A multiple case study design can engage the researcher in exploring, identifying, and interpreting qualities, behaviors, and traits within diverse samples of leaders and managers (Sadvandi & Halkias, 2019). It is further possible with the multiple case study design to understand leadership's context through participants' perceptions as a stand-alone case or through groups and organizations.

The rich detail offered by multiple case study participants is an added value to our further understanding of a myriad of management themes such as governance, technology, digital innovation and transformation, talent acquisition for competitive advantage, diverse employee groups, managing a black swan event, doing business in a conflict zone, or driving sustainable entrepreneurship across a variety of industry sectors. Data coding, theme identification, and cross-case analysis work within the multiple case study design to capture specific management and leadership themes in ongoing scholarly investigations are described in detail within this book.

The question of how much to focus on the data rather than theory remains an issue in writing case-based research. The fact that a researcher must work within publisher-prescribed spatial constraints translates to a trade-off between presenting the empirically based data that supports the emergent theoretical framework and providing a description of that framework. This tension is further pronounced with multiple case research, given more cases, not just a single one. The best way to resolve this issue and keep a balance between "better stories" and

DOI: 10.4324/9781003244936-10

"better theories" is for the multiple case researcher to frame the paper concerning the theory and then support it with empirical evidence as exhibited by some of the cases (Eisenhardt & Graebner, 2007).

The researcher can use figures, tables, and appendices to offer an exact visual representation of a multiple case study's data analysis process (e.g., Hannah & Eisenhardt, 2018; McDonald & Gao, 2019). Single case studies do not have as many constraints as multiple case studies. In this case, a researcher often frames their paper as the case narrative and follows this with the theory. Although various written formats can be utilized, the researcher must link supporting empirical data to individual constructs and present theoretical logic underlying relationships. The best multiple case studies focus on results termed as "novel" with "discrepant data" that present a rival interpretation of the data collected from the literature, often driving implications and recommendations emanating from the study to support theory extension.

Publishing Research

At the end of any academic research, a natural step is disseminating the results of the greater academic and professional communities to inform and invite critique. Only when repeated efforts to challenge the research findings fail can we say with some certainty that the findings contribute to our understanding of the phenomenon under investigation until new research proves otherwise. Dissemination in academia is traditionally done through conference presentations and academic publications (journals, books, etc.). The latter has been supplemented with online repositories (like arXiv.org, ssrn.com, and researchgate.net), where even preliminary findings can be presented to invite feedback that will further guide the efforts of researchers.

The most popular options available for publishing research include peer-reviewed academic journals, conference proceedings, and academic research books (not to be confused with textbooks). Readers should consult the specific publisher's guidelines for other dissemination forms like newsletters, commentaries, etc. The journal and conference proceedings generally follow the same style and formatting rules; conference proceedings are often published as special issues of journals or academic research books.

When it comes to book publishing, some publishers might request a specific style, but it is generally left to the editor (for conferences) or the lead author for academic research books for the structure and style of the print material. For this reason, the details of book publishing are left for the researcher to explore through publishers' websites.

Book publishers dedicated to academic research include Routledge and Springer. Prestigious institutions like MIT and Oxford University tend to have their own publishing houses, so interested authors can find details about what they accept for publication, and how, on their respective websites. One particular case of publication, the research dissertation, will be discussed here as it is of great interest and probably the starting point for many researchers. Dissertations almost always are written in a research book style and often end up published as books.

Journal Publication

This section focuses on the form and requirements generally expected when researchers are interested in publishing in peer-reviewed academic journals. These journals are produced by major publishers like Taylor & Francis, Pearson, Springer, and Elsevier, usually on behalf of associations or groups of scientists, or by the associations themselves, such as the Institute of Electrical and Electronics Engineers (IEEE), or the American Psychological Association (APA). There is usually an Editor in Chief with Associate Editors for specialized needs and a board of reviewers that usually covers the field's breadth and depth that the journal is covering. Their primary function is to screen the material that will be published for appropriateness for the journal domain and ensure the journal structure is followed and the submissions pass the scientific rigor of the review process. The latter is usually through a double-blind review process whereby the editors assign two reviewers to anonymously evaluate the submitted material (frequently stripped of any author details).

Based on a review process outcome, authors submitting material are informed whether their work has been accepted for publication by the journal, whether revisions are required before publication, or if it has been rejected. For prospective authors, even when their work is rejected, there is value as they receive feedback from the paper reviewers on the areas that were not appropriately covered and supported. This way, researchers can learn from each other and improve the quality of their research.

Prospective authors can find the details of the publication process from the journal's website and additional information about the journal submission's success rates and possibly categorize the journal's popularity as a source for references by the researcher. This is usually indicated by calculating an impact factor metric that some organizations like Thomson Reuters produce for academic journals. They can range from 0 to even high numbers (40 and above) for a few select journals, but the great majority of journals will fall below 10, with the most probable values around 3 and even lower.

This is not by far a fair process, as quality work can be found even in journals with impact factors below 1, but as in any social function, tradition, prestige, and even politics in the form of author affiliations can carry a long way to publication. Having a prestigious journal name may draw initial attention to someone's research, but by far what will make research "famous" is the quality of the work presented and its dissemination by the researcher in more interactive and engaging modes like conferences, presentations, and, nowadays, bulletin and discussion boards/groups in professional associations and social network sites.

While the material that will follow here covers the general requirements in terms of style and structure in most academic journals, researchers should always check the specific requirements set by their target journal (usually found on the journal's website). Another point of reference for the discussion is that we mainly focus on original research (excluding newsletters, commentaries, etc.) and social sciences research. However, other research fields' deviations should be minimal and usually concern the citation style and formatting.

A uniform style is found primarily to do with convenience when reviewing research papers, as we can quickly locate the sections that are of interest to us and retrieve critical points and findings. Style helps express the key elements of quantitative research (like statistics, tables, graphs, etc.) in a consistent way that allows retrieval and processing without distractions. This also provides clarity in communication and allows researchers to focus on the substance of their research. Research paper styles have been recommended by major scientific bodies like APA, developed by the American Psychological Association, but in general, what is known as the IMRaD (Introduction, Methods, Results, and Discussion) structure is the standard many journals follow with minor deviations like separating the review of the literature from the introduction. We have a complete journal publication structure if we add the title page at the beginning and the references at the end.

Before we proceed with a discussion of the structure mentioned above, it is worth pointing out that occasionally journals will impose a word count limit on the length of a manuscript mainly due to space restriction in the journal and to restrain authors from getting "carried away" with their presentation. Typical size limits are set at around 10,000 words or less. Presumably, if more is required, the authors should consider alternative routes like publishing their research as a book. Many publishers specialize in such publications and encourage authors to publish their research, even collecting similar research, like conference proceedings.

Title Page

Every published work comes with a title that identifies the work and conveys its context as much as possible. Titles summarize the following work and should be concise about the topic, the variables and constructs involved, and their relationships. At the same time, titles should be able to stand alone as representatives of the whole research. In this respect, titles in the form of questions are not widespread and, when used, suggest all the above. There are no specific guidelines regarding the title's length but typically average between 10 and 15 words. Following the research title, we usually have the names, affiliations, and contact details of the published authors with markings for the corresponding author who is available to answer queries and follow up with the published material.

The next piece of information that follows is the abstract of the research. This is a one-paragraph summary of the contents of the research. It includes the phenomenon under investigation, the study's essential features like its methodology and research design, the profile of the study population, and the sampling process used. This should be followed by the basic findings, including metrics like statistical significance, confidence intervals, effect sizes, etc., and the research's main conclusions. In essence, the abstract is a compressed IMRaD.

A typical breakdown of the extent of the various sections in an abstract (for those journals that do not force the breakdown) could be 25% Introduction, 25% Methods, 35% Results, and 15% Discussion. In terms of length, typical abstract requirements range between 150 and 250 words. Like the title, the abstract should stand on its own if separated from the rest of the paper. Abstracts tend to be available for free as promotional material and, as such, are freely distributed.

Following the abstract narrative, a keyword section is required. This usually contains a list of four to six keywords that identify the research area and can be used for indexing purposes. Usually, these are the keywords we would expect someone to use to find our research in a search engine.

IMRaD Sections

The core of a research publication starts with the introduction. As in most writing types, we begin by explaining what problem is studied and why it is/was necessary to research it. For applied research, this might present the need for understanding or solving a social problem, while theoretical research (frequently referred to as basic research) might concern the development of theory or extension of existing theory to new cases. Our discussion should be as neutral as possible, presenting arguments from all sides of the debate. The introduction needs to build up the case for the problem the research will address.

If the journal strictly adheres to the IMRaD standard, we need to present a review of the literature related to our research subject. If not, then basic references to the specific subject will need to be briefly mentioned at this stage. The current state of the research field is presented with an emphasis on "gaps" that need to be addressed with additional research. The material should be presented as proof of the timeliness and necessity for addressing the gap through our research.

A point of interest here is that a literature gap is not a sufficient reason as there are infinite gaps that might not be of great importance to humanity at this time of our evolution. For example, there is a gap in the academic literature on alien societies, but we can be assured that unless we have regular encounters with aliens, the subject will be of very little importance to our societies (excluding probably to those individuals who claim to have been abducted by aliens). The gap supports the study's significance, but it should not dominate the importance of the study that is primarily its contribution to theory, practice, or both.

This discussion should be followed by a clear statement of our research's purpose (obviously to address the problem raised in the previous material) with a detailed list of the hypotheses we formed and their appropriateness to the research design. In some cases, the hypotheses might be preceded by the research questions used to create them, but most quantitative journal publications will skip the research questions as the hypotheses can directly imply them. Both research questions and hypotheses will need to show their relevance to the theory and the constructs used as the research framework and should be a natural and logical outcome of the previous discussion.

Having discussed what our research is all about, we move on to discussing what the research did. This is where the various theoretical constructs and variables will be operationalized, and a detailed description of the methods used will be discussed. The details should be sufficient for other researchers to replicate and confirm or disprove our study's findings. Readers should also have sufficient information to evaluate the appropriateness of the methods we used for the hypotheses we set and the type of data we collected. References to past research that used similar methods for similar studies should support our choices. It is suggested that the methods/methodology section be written in the past tense and passive voice to reduce researcher biases when discussing their choices (depersonalizing the presentation).

After the methods, we proceed to the results section, summarize the collected data, the analysis we performed on them, and our research results. This needs to be done in sufficient detail to provide a complete picture of the results to someone with professional knowledge of quantitative methods. No citations for the methods used are necessary for this section unless a justification for a particular procedure is required to interpret the results. The language used in reporting statistical results is more or less standard, so we will provide a list of how such results could be presented.

After presenting the results, we come to the last main section to discuss the research findings. This section is often titled "Conclusions and Recommendations." At this stage, we should evaluate and interpret the results in light of the hypotheses we adopted. This means accepting or rejecting hypotheses and presenting a rational explanation for the decision and its implications on the research topic. Further, the discussion needs to compare our research findings with past findings that could support or oppose our results and explain potential similarities and differences. Biases, assumptions, and limitations that we acknowledged should be addressed in our validity and reliability analysis. The discussion section should end with a well-supported commentary on the findings' importance, and the direction future research efforts should take to confirm and expand our research. This is important as future researchers will use it as a basis upon which they will justify the need for their research in the same area.

References

The last part of a journal publication is, if not the most, "torturous," for sure the most boring one (based on anecdotal evidence and personal experience). Citing research work and referencing is a requirement for every research publication as it provides the sources used to make statements about claims and facts related to our research in some way. By the time researchers reach this stage, they will have undoubtedly seen hundreds of citation and reference styles by reviewing the literature they have conducted, so some familiarity with referencing styles will have been picked up along the way.

Popular styles nowadays include the American Psychological Association (APA), Modern Language Association (MLA), Institute of Electrical and Electronics Engineers (IEEE), Chicago Manual of Style, and Harvard. Different associations and journals have developed these to ensure compliance and in addressing the needs of specific disciplines.

APA, for example, is predominantly used in social sciences, while IEEE is very popular in engineering and sciences. Overall, there are remarkable similarities between them as they all need to describe the source material sufficiently, but the differences could be enough to lead to paper rejection if not adequately addressed. For additional referencing and in-text citation styles, the reader should refer to websites explaining various styles.

Luckily for researchers, there is software that has been developed to manage references. Zotero is a popular free software with a citation manager and plugins for browsers like Firefox, Chrome, and Microsoft Word. It allows for the creation of a citation library that multiple researchers can access and update online. It can also produce a bibliography in any of the popular formats available. Similar functionality is provided by other products like RefWorks and Mendeley. Interested researchers should spend some time familiarizing themselves with such products as they are one of the best investments of time one can afford for academic publishing.

Dissertations and Theses

A particular category of published research is that of doctoral dissertations. These can be at the master's level (M.Sc., M.Ed., MFA, etc.) or the doctorate level (Ph.D., DBA, Ed.D., D.Eng., etc.). The differences are mainly in the length of the manuscript (with the doctorate being more extended), which generally reflects the amount of time dedicated to the degree (1–2 years for MS and 3+ additional years for the doctorate) and the contribution of the work to theory (this is mainly the Ph.D. domain) and practice (mainly DBA and MS domain).

The great majority of dissertations follow a standard five-chapter structure in the IMRaD format with the interjection of a literature chapter after the introduction deemed necessary due to the extensive coverage of a dissertation's research topic regarding what has been done in the past. The reader should keep in mind that additional entries are required before these chapters and include:

- **Title** page: include the research title, type of degree, school and department, author name, and publication year.
- **Abstract** page.
- **Acknowledgments** page: everyone who has contributed to the research should be acknowledged here in any form or means.
- **Table of Contents** page.

- **List of Tables** page: should mirror table titles within the paper's body according to the school's referencing style.
- **List of Figures** page: should mirror figure titles according to the school's referencing style.

The five chapters are followed by the references section and any appendices mentioned in the text's main body. When the dissertation is complete and has been successfully defended, the researcher can proceed with the publication process. Besides publishing it as a printed book, dedicated databases like ProQuest accept dissertations and make them available to anyone interested.

11 Concluding Thoughts

Researchers develop *case studies* to bring a complex topic closer to a broader audience. Case studies provide a means for highlighting and extracting practical principles and methods for shaping progress in solving real-world problems. Case study research is now considered a mainstream methodological approach in contemporary research; it has a long tradition within the broad area of social science and organizational strategy, management, and leadership studies. A well-constructed multiple case study design can provide a reliable theory extension that is internally coherent, accurate, robust, and parsimonious. Extension studies are essential in the scholarly literature and not only because they provide replication evidence. Multiple case study research results can extend theory and knowledge within conceptual frameworks from previous studies' results in new and theoretically essential directions.

A multiple case study is a potentially valuable means of capturing the complexity of a phenomenon while revealing rich understandings about the context in which it is based. In terms of costs, a multiple case study can be one of the most expensive ways of investigating due to the research's time- and labor-intensive nature. Because the researchers are the main instrument in multiple case studies, they need to be well prepared for the fieldwork requirements. This preparation includes being able to make analytical judgments while collecting data.

A qualitative multiple case study allows the in-depth study of holistic and meaningful characteristics of real-life events. It can explain the underlying forces that support relationships and answer how and why those relationships are sustained. When the study aims to include making an original contribution to a theoretical or conceptual framework and provide a rich, powerful picture of human interaction, a multiple case study approach is recommended over a single case study. The cases are analyzed using replication logic to offer contrasts between each case and extend theoretical constructs. The qualitative method

DOI: 10.4324/9781003244936-11

allows probing questions using various data sources, contributing to the study's originality.

To address a study's problem, the multiple case study design and the selection of the cases are categorized into two types: the *literal replication* and the *theoretical replication*. While the former means that case studies selected yield similar results, the latter means that case studies are selected to predict contradictory results. In a multiple case study, the "case" itself may be a person, event, entity, or another unit of analysis (Yin, 2017). Nevertheless, the most rigorous multiple case studies focus on theory extension. Critical research skill is understanding how to write up theory extensions from multiple case studies that are high-quality and rigorous and know how to evaluate this research. Two critical points to remember: (1) rather than extending theory through formulaic data analysis schemes, replication is at the heart of multi-case theory extension; and (2) the aim of such research is the insight into a phenomenon, not theory-testing.

Most organizations at present exist in volatile economic and social environments across developed and developing markets (Neubert, 2018). Today's leaders and managers face unforeseen and, at times, unimaginable challenges and are called upon to provide innovative and sustainable directions by their organizational stakeholders. The future of local, regional, and global business is uncertain at best. Case study researchers will continue to play a pivotal role in offering a voice as to how people, places, and events continually shape and reshape today's business and technology transactions across nations' regional and local communities. Exploring leaders' and managers' behaviors within global and local contexts using the multiple case study design provides valuable insight into how and why leadership and management of people and organizations will be the compass leading toward the future global economy.

References

Abadir, S., Batsa, E. T., Neubert, M., & Halkias, D. (2020). *Leading multicultural teams in agile organizations.* Available at https://papers.ssrn.com/sol3/papers.cfm?abstract_id=3507635

Anney, V. N. (2014). Ensuring the quality of the findings of qualitative research: Looking at trustworthiness criteria. *Journal of Emerging Trends in Educational Research and Policy Studies, 5*(2), 272–281.

Baškarada, S., & Koronios, A. (2017). Unicorn data scientist: The rarest of breeds. *Program: electronic library and information systems, 51*(1), 65–74. https://doi.org/10.1108/PROG-07-2016-0053

Baxter, P., & Jack, S. (2008). Qualitative case study methodology: Study design and implementation for novice researchers. *The Qualitative Report, 13*(4), 544–559. https://doi.org/10.46743/2160-3715/2008.1573

Benoot, C., Hannes, K., & Bilsen, J. (2016). The use of purposeful sampling in a qualitative evidence synthesis: A worked example on sexual adjustment to a cancer trajectory. *BMC Medical Research Methodology, 16*(1), Article 21. https://doi.org/10.1186/s12874-016-0114-6

Bonett, D. G. (2012). Replication-extension studies. *Current Directions in Psychological Science, 21*(6), 409–412. https://doi.org/10.1177%2F0963721412459512

Brown Jr, W. L. (2017). *Airport managers' perspectives on security and safety management systems in aviation operations: A multiple case study* (Publication No. AAT 10259101) [Doctoral dissertation, Northcentral University]. ProQuest Dissertations & Theses.

Burns, R. B. (2000). *Introduction to research methods.* Sage Publications.

Collins, C. S., & Stockton, C. M. (2018). The central role of theory in qualitative research. *International Journal of Qualitative Methods, 17*(1). https://doi.org/10.1177/1609406918797475

Cooper, K., & White, R. E. (2012). *Qualitative research in the post-modern era: Contexts of qualitative research.* Springer.

Denzin, N. K., & Lincoln, Y. S. (2005). Introduction. The discipline and practice of qualitative research. In N. K. Denzin & Y. S. Lincoln (Eds.), *The SAGE handbook of qualitative research* (3rd ed.) (pp. 1–32). Sage Publications.

Eisenhardt, K. M. (1989). Building theories from case study research. *Academy of Management Review, 14*(4), 532–550. https://doi.org/10.5465/amr.1989.4308385

Eisenhardt, K. M. (2020). Theorizing from cases: A commentary. In L. Eden, B. Nielsen, & A. Verbeke (Eds.), *Research methods in international business* (pp. 221–227). JIBS Special Collections. Palgrave Macmillan. https://doi.org/10.1007/978-3-030-22113-3_10

Eisenhardt, K. M., & Graebner, M. E. (2007). Theory building from cases: Opportunities and challenges. *Academy of Management Journal, 50*(1), 25–32. https://doi.org/10.5465/amj.2007.24160888

Fiss, P. C. (2009). Case studies and the configurational analysis of organizational phenomena. In *The SAGE handbook of case-based methods* (pp. 424–440). Sage Publications. www.doi.org/10.4135/9781446249413

Flick, U. (2009). *An introduction to qualitative research* (4th ed.). Sage Publications.

Gelinas, L., Pierce, R., Winkler, S., Cohen, I. G., Fernandez Lynch, H., & Bierer, B. E. (2017). Using social media as a research recruitment tool: Ethical issues and recommendations. *The American Journal of Bioethics, 17*(3), 3–14. https://doi.org/10.1080/15265161.2016.1276644

Gomm, R., Hammersley, M., & Foster, P. (2000). *Case study method. Key issues, key texts.* Sage Publications.

Gray, D. E. (2019). *Doing research in the business world.* Sage Publications.

Guba, E. G., & Lincoln, Y. S. (1989). *Fourth generation evaluation.* Sage Publications.

Guba, E. G., & Lincoln, Y. S. (1994). Competing paradigms in qualitative research. In N. K. Denzin & Y. S. Lincoln (Eds.), *Handbook of qualitative research* (pp. 105–117). Sage Publications.

Guion, L. A., Diehl, D. C., & McDonald, D. (2011). *Triangulation: Establishing the validity of qualitative studies* (Publication no. FCS6014). University of Florida, IFAS Extension. https://sites.duke.edu/niou/files/2014/07/W13-Guion-2002-Triangulation-Establishing-the-Validity-of-Qualitative-Research.pdf

Halkias, D. & Neubert, M. (2020). Extension of theory in management and leadership studies using the multiple case study design. *International Leadership Journal, 12*(2), 48–73. http://internationalleadershipjournal.com/index.php/archives/

Halkias, D., Santora, J., Harkiolakis, N., & Thurman, P. (2017). *Leadership and change management: A cross-cultural perspective.* Routledge/Taylor Francis.

Hall, J. C. (2017). No longer invisible: Understanding the psychosocial impact of skin color stratification in the lives of African American women. *Health & Social Work, 42*(2), 71–78. https://doi.org/10.1093/hsw/hlx001

Hannah, D. P., & Eisenhardt, K. M. (2018). How firms navigate cooperation and competition in nascent ecosystems. *Strategic Management Journal, 39*(12), 3163–3192. https://doi.org/10.1002/smj.2750

Harkiolakis, N. (2017). *Quantitative research methods: From theory to publication.* CreateSpace.

HBP Editors. (2020, December 16). *How to teach any case online. Become the 'Author' of each case study you use in your virtual classroom.* Harvard Business Publishing. https://hbsp.harvard.edu/inspiring-minds/how-to-teach-any-business-case-study-online

HBP Editors. (2021, April 13). *The art of the case method. Part 3: Exploring the instructor's choreographic role in case-method teaching.* Harvard Business Publishing. https://hbsp.harvard.edu/inspiring-minds/the-art-of-the-case-method-centennial-part-3

Howard, D. L., Halkias, D., & Dean, H. (2019). *Women's entrepreneurial leadership practices and enterprise longevity: An integrative literature review.* https://ssrn.com/abstract=3355595

Klenke, K. (2016). Qualitative interviewing in leadership research. *Qualitative Research in the Study of Leadership,* 123–150. https://doi.org/10.1108/978-1-78560-651-920152007

Komodromos, M. (2014). Employees' perceptions of trust using an organizational justice framework in a media organization in Cyprus. *International Journal of Teaching and Case Studies, 5*(2), 158–174. https://doi.org/10.1504/IJTCS.2014.065625

Kozinets, R. V. (2015). *Netnography: Redefined* (2nd ed.). Sage Publications.

Lincoln Y. S., & Guba E. G. (1985) *Naturalistic inquiry.* Sage Publications.

Lincoln, Y. S., & Guba, E. G. (1986). But is it rigorous? Trustworthiness and authenticity in naturalistic evaluation. *New Directions for Program Evaluation, 1986*(30), 73–84. https://doi.org/10.1002/ev.1427

Livingston, R. W., Rosette, A. S., & Washington, E. F. (2012). Can an agentic black woman get ahead? The impact of race and interpersonal dominance on perceptions of female leaders. *Psychological Science, 23*(4), 354–358. https://doi.org/10.1177/0956797611428079

Marshall, C., & Rossman, G. B. (2011). *Designing qualitative research* (5th ed.). Sage Publications.

Marshall, C., & Rossman, G. B. (2016). *Designing qualitative research* (6th ed.). Sage Publications.

Mason, J. (2002). *Researching your own practice: The discipline of noticing.* Psychology Press.

Maxwell, J. A. (2012). *Qualitative research design. An interactive approach* (3rd ed.). Sage Publications.

McDonald, R., & Gao, C. (2019). Pivoting isn't enough? Managing strategic reorientation in new ventures. *Organization Science, 30*(6), 1289–1318. www.hbs.edu/faculty/Pages/item.aspx?num=55811

Merriam, S. B. (2009). *Qualitative research: A guide to design and implementation.* Jossey-Bass.

Merriam, S. B., & Grenier, R. S. (Eds.) (2019). *Qualitative research in practice: Examples for discussion and analysis* (2nd ed.). Jossey-Bass.

Merriam, S. B., & Tisdell, E. J. (2015). *Qualitative research: A guide to design and implementation.* John Wiley & Sons.

Miles, M. B., Huberman, A. M., & Saldaña, J. (2014). *Qualitative data analysis: A methods sourcebook* (3rd ed.). Sage Publications.

Miles, M. B., Huberman, A. M., & Saldaña, J. (2019). *Qualitative data analysis: A methods sourcebook* (4th ed.). Sage Publications.

Muhammad, R. (2018). *African American women managers' experiences in predominantly black work environments* (Publication No. 5504) [Doctoral dissertation, Walden University]. Walden Dissertations and Doctoral Studies. https://scholarworks.waldenu.edu/dissertations/5504

Mullen-Rhoads, R., Halkias, D., & Harkiolakis, N. (2018). Perceived challenges of e-negotiations between Chinese and American business leaders: A multiple case study. *International Leadership Journal, 10*(2), 5–17. http://internationalleadershipjournal.com/index.php/archives/summer-2018-vol-10-no-2/

National Commission for the Protection of Human Subjects of Biomedical and Behavioral Research. (1978). *The Belmont Report: Ethical principles and guidelines for the protection of human subjects of research.* U.S. Department of Health & Human Services. www.hhs.gov/ohrp/regulations-and-policy/belmont-report/read-the-belmont-report

National Research Council. (2002). *Scientific research in education.* The National Academies Press. https://doi.org/10.17226/10236

Neubert, M. (2016). Significance of the speed of internationalization for born global firms: A multiple case study approach. *International Journal of Teaching and Case Studies, 7*(1), 66–81. https://doi.org/10.1504/IJTCS.2016.076067

Neubert, M. (2018). Internationalization behavior of small and medium-sized enterprises from emerging markets: Implications for sustainability. *Latin American Journal of Management for Sustainable Development, 4*(3), 226–238. https://doi.org/10.1504/LAJMSD.2018.096072

Neubert, M., Rams, W., & Utikal, H. (2020). Experiential learning with live case studies. *International Journal of Teaching and Case Studies, 11*(2), 173–190. http://dx.doi.org/10.1504/IJTCS.2020.109726

Nonthaleerak, P., & Hendry, L. (2008). Exploring the Six Sigma phenomenon using multiple case study evidence. *International Journal of Operations & Production Management, 28*(3), 279–303. https://doi.org/10.1108/01443570810856198

Noor, K. B. M. (2008). Case study: A strategic research methodology. *American Journal of Applied Sciences, 5*(11), 1602–1604. https://doi.org/10.3844/ajassp.2008.1602.1604

Patton, M. Q. (1990). *Qualitative evaluation and research methods* (2nd ed.). Sage Publications.

Patton, M. Q. (2014). *Qualitative research & evaluation methods integrating theory and practice* (4th ed.). Sage Publications.

Phillips, T. L. (2012). *"Outsider within" narratives of diversity leadership: An exploratory case study of executive women of color* (UMI 3489799) [Doctoral dissertation, The George Washington University]. ProQuest Dissertations and Theses Global. www.proquest.com/docview/915748664?pq-origsite=gscholar&fromopenview=true

Rapp, A., & Ogilvie, J. (2019, June 7). *Live case studies demystified. How two professors bring real-world application to the classroom.* https://hbsp.harvard.edu/inspiring-minds/live-case-studies-demystified

Ridder, H. G. (2016). *Case study research. Approaches, methods, contribution to theory. Sozialwissenschaftliche Forschungsmethoden* (Vol. 12). Rainer Hampp Verlag.

Ridder, H. G. (2017). The theory contribution of case study research designs. *Business Research, 10*(2), 281–305. https://doi.org/10.1007/s40685-017-0045-z

Rosette, A. S., Zhou Koval, C., Ma, A., & Livingston, R. (2016). Race matters for women leaders: Intersectional effects on agentic deficiencies and penalties. *The Leadership Quarterly, 27*(3), 429–445. https://doi.org/10.1016/j.leaqua.2016.01.008

Sadvandi, S., & Halkias, D. (2019). Challenges of human factors engineering in the coming transition to autonomous vehicle technologies: A multiple case study. *ISM Journal of International Business, 3*(1), 3–7. www.ism.edu/ism-insights/challenges-of-human-factors-engineering-in-the-coming-transition-to-autonomous-vehicle-technologies-a-multiple-case-study.html

Saldaña, J. (2015). *The coding manual for qualitative researchers* (3rd ed.). Sage Publications.

Saldaña, J., & Omasta, M. (2018). *Qualitative research: Analyzing life.* Sage Publications.

Sanders Muhammad, R. (2020). African American women managers' experiences in predominantly black work environments: A multiple case study. *International Journal of Teaching and Case Studies, 11*(3), 133–156. https://doi.org/10.1504/IJTCS.2020.109722

Sanders Muhammad, R., & Halkias, D. (2019). African American women managers' experiences in predominantly black work environments. In *Academy of Management Proceedings, 2019*(1), Article 13154. https://journals.aom.org/doi/10.5465/AMBPP.2019.13154abstract

Schram, S. (2006). *Making political science matter: Debating knowledge, research, and method.* NYU Press.

Selsor, W. K. (2020). *Managerial competencies driving successful change initiatives: A multiple case study of healthcare administrators* (Publication No. 9255) [Doctoral dissertation, Walden University]. Walden Dissertations and Doctoral Studies. https://scholarworks.waldenu.edu/dissertations/9255

Shepherd, E. (2020). *A multicase study of critical success factors of self-service business intelligence initiatives* (Publication No. 10002) [Doctoral dissertation, Walden University]. Walden Dissertations and Doctoral Studies. https://scholarworks.waldenu.edu/dissertations/10002

Stake, R. E. (2005). *Qualitative case studies.* The Guilford Press.

Stake, R. E. (2010). *Qualitative research: Studying how things work.* The Guilford Press.

Stake, R. E. (2013). *Multiple case study analysis.* The Guilford Press.

68   References

Tsang, E. W. (2013). Case study methodology: Causal explanation, contextualization, and theorizing. *Journal of International Management, 19*(2), 195–202. https://doi.org/10.1016/j.intman.2012.08.004

Welch, C., Piekkari, R., Plakoyiannaki, E., & Paavilainen-Mäntymäki, E. (2020). Theorizing from case studies: Towards a pluralist future for international business research. In L. Eden, B. Nielsen, & A. Verbeke (Eds.), *Research methods in international business* (pp. 171–220). JIBS Special Collections. Palgrave Macmillan. https://doi.org/10.1007/978-3-030-22113-3_9

Yawar, S. A., & Seuring, S. (2017). Management of social issues in supply chains: A literature review exploring social issues, actions and performance outcomes. *Journal of Business Ethics, 141*(3), 621–643. https://doi.org/10.1007/s10551-015-2719-9

Yin, R. K. (2012). *Applications of case study methods.* Sage Publications.

Yin, R. K. (2017). *Case study research and applications: Design and methods* (6th ed.). Sage Publications.

Index

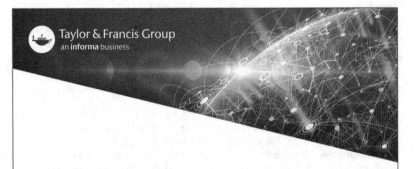

Printed in the United States
by Baker & Taylor Publisher Services